HANDBOOK FOR A POSITIVE REVOLUTION

THE FIVE SUCCESS PRINCIPLES FOR PERSONAL AND GLOBAL CHANGE

Edward de Bono

Vermilion
LONDON

1 3 5 7 9 10 8 6 4 2

Vermilion, an imprint of Ebury Publishing,
20 Vauxhall Bridge Road,
London SW1V 2SA

Vermilion is part of the Penguin Random House group of companies
whose addresses can be found at global.penguinrandomhouse.com

Penguin
Random House
UK

Published with permission from de Bono Global Pty Ltd
www.debono.com

This edition first published in the United Kingdom by
Vermilion in 2018

www.penguin.co.uk

A CIP catalogue record for this book is available from the British Library

ISBN 9781785041907

Typeset in 10.5/14.1 pt Sabon LT Std
by Integra Software Services Pvt. Ltd, Pondicherry

Printed and bound in Great Britain by Clays Ltd, Elcograf S.p.A.

Penguin Random House is committed to a sustainable future for our
business, our readers and our planet. This book is made from
Forest Stewardship Council® certified paper.

Edward de Bono is the leading authority in the field of creative thinking and originator of the term 'lateral thinking' and the ix Thinking Hats. Highly regarded internationally, his instrucion has been sought by governments, schools and leading orporations around the world.

De Bono's thinking methods provide practical, creative tools) make it possible for anyone – not just people considered arty' – to be creative on demand. These are based on an undertanding of the logic of the brain's self-organizing information ystem, which forms asymmetric patterns. This is why creative hinking can be seen as a formal and deliberate skill and not a mysterious talent. De Bono's system of lateral thinking is o powerful that the use of just one of his methods produced 1,000 ideas in a single afternoon at a workshop with a steel company.

In the Middle Ages the influence of the Church gave rise) good thinking for finding the truth, which in turn served us ell in science. Edward de Bono believes this is 'ebne' (excellent it not enough). Culturally, we have never developed thinking r creating value but it is now time we treated it much more s riously. As part of this initiative Edward de Bono has taught th nking directly in schools and his methods are in use in thou ds of schools worldwide. Research has shown improvement ll subjects, increased employment and much-reduced crimi behaviour.

dward de Bono holds an MD (Malta), MA (Oxford), DPhil ford), PhD (Cambridge) and Ddes (RMIT). He has had lty appointments at the universities of Oxford, Cambridge, lon and Harvard and was a Rhodes Scholar at Oxford. He written 83 books, translated into 42 languages, in the field of creativity and thinking, including the global bestsellers *Six Thinking Hats* and *Lateral Thinking*.

CONTENTS

EDITOR'S NOTE

Edward de Bono is the leading authority in the field of creative thinking and the publishers are delighted to be bringing this thought-provoking work back into print.

The author was writing in a different political and social era, and many of the examples he cites offer a snapshot of this time. However, though there have been considerable changes – politically, socially and economically – over the last thirty years or so, this important book explores key issues which still require attention, even in today's fast-paced world, and many parallels can be drawn with life today. The fundamental principles and themes in this book will encourage us to change the way we think; as the author himself says, 'In a rapidly changing world we are finding that our thinking is inadequate to meet the demands put on it'.

Edward de Bono's teaching is as valid today as when this book was first published, and will resonate with readers for many years to come.

AUTHOR'S NOTE

Why bother? This is a sensible phrase to cover a sensible strategy. Go your own way. Do your own thing. Carve out a little niche in the complex world and then be happy and content in that niche. Being worried about the rest of the world is too futile and too difficult a task. Let those who are motivated to change the world work on that task. The world will always last long enough to see out your lifetime.

I am not going to disagree with this point of view but sidestep it in order to write for those who know that they are inseparably part of the world in which they live: their own internal world, the local community world and the world at large. Let the others munch contentedly like cows in the field, happy that there is grass today.

My concern has always been with human thinking because this seems to me to play so central a role in human happiness and development both from moment-to-moment and also over the longer term. I believe that we have done relatively little about thinking but have been content with a fluency of argument and the ability to attack and defend positions. This sort of thinking unfortunately lacks the creative, constructive and design energies that we really need in order to go forward. Indeed, our absurd emphasis on negativity seriously impedes such progress.

This particular book is not, however, about thinking habits and methods. This book is about the fundamental background and setting in which we would use our thinking skills. If we are disposed to be negative then our thinking skills will help us to be negative. If we are disposed to be positive then our thinking skills will take us in that direction. This is more than a moment-to-moment emotional bias – it is the fundamental attitude of our being.

There are far too many people who believe that natural evolution controlled by critical negativity will form the ideas that we need – just as Darwinian evolution perfected a variety of life forms. This is a dangerous fallacy. Evolution is very slow, very messy, very wasteful and is incapable of making the best use of available resources. Inadequate – but not disastrous – ideas and institutions will survive, perfect and defend themselves thus preventing the more effective use of resources. That has always been the logical basis for revolution.

This book is intended for those who see this logical need.

There is a useful place for negativity in changing values: in providing shaping pressures; in curbing excesses; in removing defects in order to improve an idea; and in forming the conscience of society. But the constructive and creative energies have to be there in order to get the steady, step-by-step progress that is the basis of the positive revolution. How we generate these constructive energies is what the positive revolution is about.

INTRODUCTION

This is a serious revolutionary handbook. The greatest strength of this serious revolution is that it will not be taken seriously. There is no greater power than to be effective and not to be taken seriously. That way you can quietly get on with things without the fuss and friction or resistance from those who feel threatened.

In the positive revolution there are no enemies. Traditional revolutions are negative and derive their energy from being against things. The only energy of the Marxist revolution was derived from its struggle against capitalism. Where that struggle was successful, the new system eventually died of inertia since the struggle becomes only an ancestral memory.

Is it possible to have a revolution without the rage, hatred and passion of being 'against' something? Is it possible to have a revolution without the sense of mission and focused energy that an 'enemy' provides? Many would say that it is not possible. Such people are locked into that old-fashioned and tiresome habit of thinking based on 'I am right – you are wrong.'

Righteousness is indeed a traditional source of energy. A simplistic view of an enemy does give the cohesion, shared views and camaraderie of professional revolutionaries. But the positive revolution is not for professional revolutionaries but for ordinary people – for those amateurs who can make a difference, inch by inch. A positive revolution is not the mighty clash of the 'rock logic' of brutally arrogant ideologies but the slow and steady power of 'water logic' with the ability to surround and infiltrate.

The weapons of the positive revolution are not bullets and bombs but simple human perceptions. Bullets and bombs may offer physical power but eventually will only work if they change perceptions and values. Why not go the direct route and work with perceptions and values?

With the positive revolution there are no enemies – even those who want to enjoy being enemies need to be denied this legitimate pleasure. There are a few who will join the positive revolution immediately. There are those who will join later when it is fashionable. There are many, including the enemies, who will be quietly bypassed. Most will not notice it is happening until it is far advanced.

I finished writing my book *I am Right, You are Wrong* one sunny summer morning at nine o'clock. Half an hour later I had started this book. This book is the short, practical, handbook for the positive revolution. The other book provides the intellectual basis and seeks to show why our traditional clash system of thinking is insufficiently constructive.

The book *I am Right, You are Wrong* was received with rather comic sputterings of indignation and hysterical outrage – directed at me for my temerity in challenging the hallowed basis of Western thinking, rather than at the substance of the book. Mostly, this quaint fury indicated how necessary it is to move forward from the traditional negativity of thinking towards the positive habits that are going to be increasingly required in the future.

This practical handbook was originally written for Brazil, which so badly needs a revolution but whose intellectuals are much too old-fashioned to design one. The book was published in Brazil, in Portuguese, at the end of 1989. This original purpose may account for some aspects of the book, particularly the need to be simple and definite. Nevertheless, the positive revolution is needed everywhere. This is particularly the case in the United Kingdom where negativity has so often been the means by which a club of mediocrity holds on to power. After reading this book, or the preceding one, some thinkers may come to see negativity not as the highest exercise of intelligence but as the squalling of a baby who has no better means of getting attention and is incapable of other action.

This book is a practical handbook and not an intellectual thesis. There are not many pages.

In writing this book I am well aware that some aspects will seem gimmicky and unnecessary. I am prepared to accept such criticism because perceptions do require to be anchored in symbols, slogans and rituals. Traditional revolutionaries have been right about this. Most successful world religions have maintained their strength through intellectually unnecessary gimmicks and rituals. Such rituals provide the continuity between bouts of emotional energy and provide the permanent seeds for the survival and dissemination of the new perceptions.

This is your personal revolutionary handbook. It is a permanent symbolic reminder of the positive revolution, not a bowl of cereal into which you dip one morning to soothe a temporary hunger. The more you invest in the positive revolution the more you will get out of it.

Is the positive revolution a personal revolution within an individual? Is the positive revolution a social revolution? Is the positive revolution a national or international revolution? You must answer that question for yourself – because it could be any or all of them.

If you want to spread the positive revolution buy a few copies of the book for your friends – or encourage them to buy the book for themselves. It is not so much a book for reading as a book for working from.

1 EFFECTIVENESS AND ACTION

If I had to design a system in which it was impossible for intelligent people to be effective, then I would design the following system:

1. People in positions of power would use their intelligence to defend their position and to survive. They would have to look after their own interests on the short-term basis that is necessary for survival. They would need all their intelligence and energy to defend themselves. Initiatives are risky because they only confirm friends and create new enemies. If this sounds a little bit like normal politics that is no coincidence or any fault of the people involved. It is the natural behaviour of the system as it is designed.

2. Intelligent people mainly use their intelligence to attack, criticize and blame others. This is easy to do and is also low-risk. This is also the highly esteemed Western tradition of 'the critical search for the truth'.

3. Everyone else is intelligent enough to be passive, to get on with their own lives and to assume that their occasional vote is a sufficient contribution to local and

world affairs. Where necessary, protest and pressure and the threat of vote switching will get things done. It is assumed that those whose business it is to get things done will respond constructively to the pressure.

Two people of matched strength are pulling on a rope in opposite directions. There is huffing and puffing and both parties are red in the face from the exertion. A great deal of energy is clearly being used. You could not, however, tell this from the position of the rope because the rope has not moved at all. In fact the whole system is perfectly static even though so much energy is actually being used.

You start up the car and try to accelerate. The car moves forward very slowly. Suddenly you realize that you have left the handbrake on.

There is no law of nature that says that energy and working hard must produce a forward or beneficial effect. Energy will only produce an effect when it is coordinated and organized towards action.

Every piece of iron can be considered to be made up of thousands of tiny magnets. All these tiny magnets are pointing in different directions – so the overall effect is zero as they pull against each other. If, however, all the tiny magnets can be lined up to point in the same direction then the piece of iron acquires the mysterious power of a magnet.

Mighty mountain ranges and landscapes are sculpted by the power of tiny drops of rain, each of which eventually comes to act in the same direction. It takes time.

Traditional negative revolutions are led by a revolutionary group. According to Lenin, who carried through a successful revolution, the power group had to lead and everyone else had to follow. Is it possible to start a revolution the other way round? Is it possible to have a general shift in mood and action first? I believe it is if the weapons are perceptions rather than bullets and bombs.

NON-ALIGNED

S **ALIGNED** N

2 NEGATIVE REVOLUTIONS

In a traditional negative revolution there is an enemy to be hated. It is this hatred which gives cohesion to the revolution and provides a sharp sense of purpose.

Traditional negative revolutions are defined by what they are attacking. In a traditional revolution you are defined as a revolutionary by what you are against: colonialism, Marxism, capitalism, tyranny, etc.

The unexpectedly sudden changes in Romania, the rest of Eastern Europe and the USSR showed that this sort of revolution can be effective and may seem to reinforce the validity of that traditional model. But there are two important factors to keep in mind. In Eastern Europe the revolutions were nationalistic revolutions against an 'occupying power'. In all cases the revolutions were against one system – Marxist economics – and towards the perceived benefits of the well-established capitalist system with its freedoms and material well-being. In other words it is relatively easy to switch, by revolution, from the existing model to another known model.

But if there is no known model to switch towards then traditional negative revolutions are pointless and dangerous. The struggle against the 'enemy' still gives a sense of mission and a purpose to life. The struggle becomes an end in itself. The revolution is only successful as a struggle and when the revolution has succeeded there is too little experience with the constructive attitude that is needed to build and to run society. The negativity that may be so valuable during the revolution is now turned inwards into fighting between the factions and, sometimes, a suppression of 'counter-revolutionaries'. The habits of negativity and attack are not suddenly changed to positive construction. That is why it might be better to start off with a positive revolution in the first place.

A positive revolution may be contrasted with a negative one:

- Instead of attack there is construction.
- Instead of criticism there is design.
- Instead of change through violence there is change through perception.
- Instead of the power of guns there is the power of information.
- Instead of the hard edges of 'rock logic' there is the now of 'water logic'.
- Instead of ideology to provide the direction there is a humour to allow changes in direction.
- Instead of a centrally organized system there is a self-organizing system.

Although the positive revolution is non-violent it is by no means passive. On the contrary, the emphasis is on action and effectiveness.

The revolution of Karl Marx was inspired by the unfairness of the steam-engine technology of the industrial revolution. The positive revolution is inspired by the opportunities offered by the electronic age of information.

3 THE POSITIVE REVOLUTION

A stool has three legs. A stool with three legs is stable on rough ground. A chair with four legs is only stable on smooth ground. A revolution has to work under difficult conditions – everything is not always smooth.

The positive revolution has three supporting legs:

1. PRINCIPLES: The basic principles are the guidelines for thinking. The basic principles set the direction for thinking and for decisions. In the positive revolution we design rather than destroy and for 'design' there must be a direction.
2. METHODS: A painter uses a paintbrush to paint. A cook uses a frying pan to cook. A carpenter uses a saw to cut wood. What are the methods and mechanisms of the positive revolution?
3. POWER: The positive revolution does not use the power of violence. It uses the power of perception, of information and of effectiveness. These powers can be used much more widely than violence.

THE PRINCIPLES

There are five basic principles of the positive revolution.

Why five?

Because there are five fingers on a hand and it is therefore easy to remember the five basic principles. The hand can also become a symbol of the revolution.

1. EFFECTIVENESS: Without effectiveness there are only dreams. Effectiveness means setting out to do something and doing it. Effectiveness is the 'thumb' on the hand, because without the thumb the hand is useless.

2. CONSTRUCTIVE: The direction of the revolution is positive not negative, constructive not destructive. This is represented by the index finger because that is the finger you use to point out the direction and the way to go.

3. RESPECT: Respect covers the way you behave towards all other human beings. Respect covers human values and human feelings. A revolution is by people but also for people – so respect is essential. This is represented by the second finger because this finger is the longest finger of the hand and respect is the most important principle of all. If you cannot be positive towards fellow human beings what is the point of being positive?

4. SELF-IMPROVEMENT: Every individual has the right, and duty, to make himself or herself better. This is both the energy of the revolution and also its purpose. A machine cannot make itself better but a human being can. This is the third finger. We do not notice this finger much – but it is there all the time. So self-improvement must also be there.

5. CONTRIBUTION: Contribution is the essence of the positive revolution. Not what you can expect or demand, but what you can contribute. If 'contribution' is so very important why does it just have the little finger on the hand? To remind us that we can contribute even if the contribution is very small. Eventually, small contributions add up to big effects.

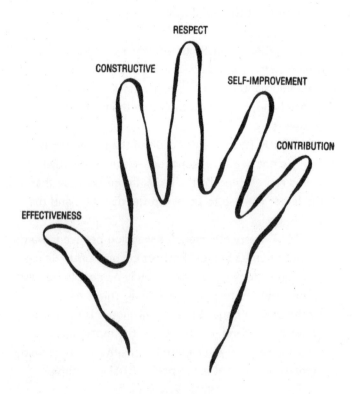

4 CONSTRUCTIVE

We must deal with the direction first because without a direction there is no revolution – just energy and grumbling.

'Constructive', represented by the index finger, is the direction.

'Constructive' can be defined in two ways: by what it is and by what it is not.

'Constructive' is the action side of 'positive'. We can feel positive about something but putting that positive feeling into action is being constructive.

A young child who puts one stone upon another is being constructive. Something new has been created. Building a house is constructive. Cooking a meal is constructive.

Constructive means action, building, making things happen – but always in the positive sense.

Energy and activity by themselves are not constructive. The example of two people pulling on a rope in opposite directions is not constructive. The energy and activity are there but nothing useful happens.

Sitting watching television for five hours is not constructive in itself. It is time-filling. Planting a seed or carving a piece of wood is constructive. The simple question is: at the end of the time, what is left? If you take exercise to keep fit that can be constructive. If you practise the guitar that can be constructive.

It is when we put together 'constructive' and 'contribution' that we begin to operate the positive revolution.

Constructive is the opposite of drift. Constructive is the opposite of passivity. Constructive is the opposite of negative. Constructive is the opposite of destructive.

Some people drift along like a cork on a river, feeling that they cannot do anything except drift, moment to moment. This is an attitude of mind. Everyone can be constructive even in tiny ways.

Some people are passive and expect everything to be done for them. Constructive is beginning to feel that you can do things yourself. Being constructive is a frame through which we look at the world. Being constructive means having positive expectations not of what may happen to you but of what you can do.

Some people enjoy being negative. They enjoy criticizing, blaming and attacking. There is a sort of self-indulgence of negativity. We must realize that being negative is easy and cheap. Being negative is not heroic or intelligent.

Socially we need to devalue critical thinking and negativity. At present we enjoy it too much and we esteem it too much. We must learn to say: 'Poor fellow, he can only be negative.'

We must put being constructive on a much higher level than being negative. But being negative is much easier because that is just talk and being constructive means doing something. But we can also be positive and constructive in our talking. For example, pointing out negativity is a way of being constructive.

Traditional revolutions are destructive. There are enemies to be attacked and destroyed. The positive revolution is constructive – there are things to be built.

The traditional revolution would say: 'You are an enemy of the people and you must be shot.' The positive revolution would say: 'You have been playing a game which has not contributed enough; now there is a different game: do you want to use your talent to take part in the new game?'

There are those who say that we must first destroy in order to build. It is true that sometimes we have to pick things apart in order to put the pieces together in a better way – but this is not the same as destruction. Destruction is dangerous and wasteful and provides nothing towards rebuilding.

What about enjoying life: friends, parties, food and drink? Is this constructive? For people to be happy and enjoy friends is certainly part of the picture. In traditional revolutions we say: 'Suffer now but when it is all over you will be happy.' The positive revolution says: 'Work the positive revolution but also be happy.' As we shall see later, humour is a key part of the positive revolution (page 53). It is when enjoying life becomes the total purpose that we fail to be constructive, or even to enjoy life. Achievement is one of life's more durable joys.

Design

The positive revolution supports design instead of criticism. Instead of saying what is wrong with something we try to say: 'How could this be done better?'

It is true that sometimes constructive criticism can remove the faults in the way something is done and so make the process better. But the attitude must be constructive.

Design sets out to put things together so that the outcome is constructive and effective. The outcome could be a meal, a house or a system of tax. Design needs the creative and constructive thinking we never teach in schools or universities because we are too busy teaching knowledge, criticism and analysis.

Once we have the right positive and constructive attitudes, and also the needed energy, then design determines how effective our actions will be. Effectiveness is one of the five basic principles of the positive revolution and we shall come to that later (page 29).

Not every action is equally effective. Energy can be wasted. So we do need to think carefully about the design of our actions.

Design is a way of focusing constructive energies on to a target. The consideration of alternatives, of objectives, of priorities and of resources available is all part of the design process.

This is worth doing and we can do it – so let us do it well.

5 CONTRIBUTION

You are walking along a street which is full of pieces of paper. Now it is possible that all that paper blew off the back of a truck carrying wastepaper. It is possible that dogs upset some dustbins and the wind blew the papers about. It is most likely that each piece of paper was casually dropped by someone. So you casually drop the wrapper of your chocolate bar. If the street is already so dirty, what difference will your additional piece make?

Or you say to yourself that it is too bad the street is dirty. It is the business of the local authority to clean the streets and they are not doing their job properly.

Now that story is the opposite of contribution. If you are following the principle of contribution you do not drop your piece of paper – whether this makes any difference or not. When enough people also do this the street becomes cleaner and easier to clean. Suppose you picked up a piece of paper: one piece, two pieces, three pieces. Should you clean the entire street? No. Just pick up a few pieces.

When you pick up these pieces of paper, how constructive are you being?

You are helping yourself by practising the attitude and discipline of contribution.

You are helping to make the street cleaner.

You are setting an example that can spread to other people.

There is a hole in the road in front of your house. You try to fill in that hole. Very soon the traffic has opened up the hole again. You fill it again. Is this a real contribution or are you wasting your time? There are three answers. You are developing your sense of contribution. Even though it is not filled permanently the hole is now filled at least part of the time. There may be a better 'design' for your contribution: finding better ways of filling the hole; putting up a sign warning drivers of the hole; informing the local authority.

The basic principle of contribution is represented by the little finger on the hand to remind us that contributions may be small but are still contributions.

The biggest difficulty with the principle of contribution is that everyone says: 'I am not in a position of power so what can I do?' That is negativity and passivity.

Nor is it enough to say: 'If I do my own job well that is enough contribution.' This is indeed an extremely important contribution – but not enough.

Suppose you kept a 'contribution diary' and at the end of the day you put down your contribution that day. One day the entry might read: Picked up a piece of paper in the street. Another day the entry might be: Helped an old woman across the street. Then there would be days with no entries at all. Would you really say to yourself: 'There was nothing that I could contribute today'? If such a diary sounds silly, ask yourself why it sounds silly.

There are three aspects of contribution:

1. The person making the contribution.
2. The person receiving the contribution.
3. The person thinking up ways of contributing.

One of the most important roles of the positive revolution is that of the 'work-packager'. This means putting together a catalogue of all the different ways in which ordinary people can contribute. There is nothing worse than having people with the time and energy to contribute but not knowing what to do. It is not easy to think of things to do there and then. The catalogue, of which there may be many, can put together the experience of people in other areas. The catalogue can be put together by a group that specifically sets out to design valuable forms of contribution.

We assume that 'work' exists and is obvious. In the future of employment one of the most important roles is going to be the 'work-packager' who designs work that can be done in order to provide value. Such work would be paid for with the normal economic currency. The contribution catalogue would be similar except that the work would be paid for with an imaginary 'care currency' which will come to exist one day.

The catalogue could include such things as the following:

- Collecting and passing on information.
- Bringing people together for a purpose.
- Explaining regulations to people and helping to fill in forms.
- Micro-education in teaching things to people willing to learn.
- Helping people who are sick or who have a disability.
- Stopping environmental pollution.
- Cleaning places up and making them more attractive.
- Preventing crime.
- Adding to the catalogue on a local level or a wider level.
- Encouraging a constructive attitude in others.
- Devaluing negativity and passivity.
- Passing on the message of this handbook to others.
- Setting up a project group or joining a project group.

Constructive achievement can become a hobby. Setting out to do something and then doing it gives a great sense of joy. It is this idea of achievement as a hobby that is the basis of the E-Clubs ('E' for Effectiveness) that are described later in this handbook (page 119).

Circles of Concern

Where do we contribute?

Imagine that there are three circles, one inside another. The innermost circle represents your self. The next circle represents your family, friends and community. The third circle represents the country and the world.

1. SELF: What are you contributing to yourself? This includes skills, education, training, experience. It also includes a positive attitude, a constructive attitude and the discipline of contributions. Self-improvement is one of the five basic principles of the positive revolution so it is an important area of contribution.

2. LOCAL: I could have suggested one circle to represent your family and your friends and another circle to represent the local community in which you live and also the community of the people with whom you work. I did not want to do this because there is already too big a gap between family and friends and the local community. So the circle includes family and friends and the local community and the work community. Your family will always be special for you and this single circle also makes your community special. There is no boundary between your family and your community.

3. COUNTRY AND WORLD: This is a big area but each country is made up of its people and the world is made up of many countries. How you vote in elections, what signals you send to politicians, how you try to make the country work, these are all matters in this third area. If you learn to read and write, that is a contribution to your country as well as yourself. If you grow more crops, that is also a contribution to the country. If there is a reduction in crime, that contributes both to the community and to the country.

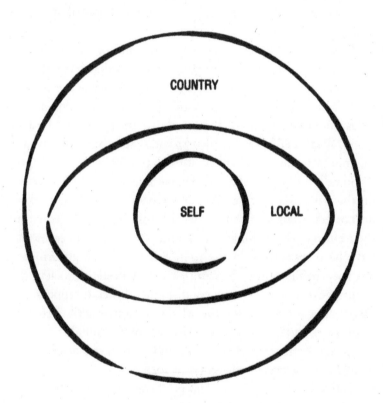

These three circles can also become another symbol of the positive revolution.

Of any action we can ask:

Is this action constructive?

To which area or areas does this action contribute?

Special Talent and Positions

Some people have a special talent and can contribute much more.

Some people are in a special position and contribute much more.

There are wealth creators. These are entrepreneurs who set up businesses or people who run businesses that have already been set up. They may be people who have inherited or bought land. Wealth creation is a valuable part of society for it provides employment, food and goods to raise the standard of living. Wealth creation can also provide the exports which earn the money to buy goods from abroad.

Some traditional revolutions have attacked wealth creators on the basis that they exploit other people and that workers do not get a fair share of the wealth that has been created by their efforts. These things are certainly true in many cases and have been more true in the past. But where the government has tried to take over the wealth-creating needs of society the results have not been very good. Some abuses disappear but others appear instead. On the whole, far less wealth is created so everyone suffers, as the Marxist economies found.

How can the talents, energies and risk-taking of entrepreneurs be harnessed for the good of society?

Here we need to use the concept of contribution. What is the business contributing in terms of: employment, taxes, quality goods, low-cost goods, profit sharing, infrastructure, training?

A business certainly has to survive in a competitive world and a business has to be profitable otherwise no one will want to put up the capital.

Risk, enterprise, organization and hard work should certainly be rewarded. The rewards should be related to the contribution. For example, profits might be related to the number of people employed and their wages. If we can solve this problem of fair reward and fair contribution then wealth creators can use their energies to create maximum wealth and contribution.

There are special talents of leadership that need to be recognized, trained and rewarded. Not everyone is able to be a leader or wants to be a leader. Leaders should be encouraged and given responsibility – provided they can show that they are constructive and can contribute. Leadership training should be part of education.

Someone once described a bureaucracy as a group of people who are brought together for a purpose but very quickly forget the purpose for which they are there. In part this is true. Many bureaucrats seem to believe that the purpose of a bureaucracy is to survive and to get paid by the government. Yet bureaucracies and the people in them should have a strong sense of contribution – both to the overall purpose and also to individual members of the public.

Some politicians also seem to play the game for its own sake: survival and continuing in power. There is some sense in this because if a politician is not in power, he or she can achieve little. So survival is important. But the point of survival is contribution.

Contribution is much more than just playing by the rules. You may stick to the rules and laws and yet contribute very little.

Contribution is a basis of judgement. Instead of saying, 'Is he or she right or wrong?', we might say: 'What is his or her contribution?'. Instead of saying, 'Is he or she good or bad?', we might say: 'What is his or her contribution?'.

Selfishness

There are people who only want to contribute to their own well-being – not even to their own self-improvement. These are the people who will cheat and exploit others. These are the people who will jump queues instead of waiting in line, and will find ways of beating the system. How should such people be treated?

Such people are often talented. The first step is to see if that talent can be used to play the new game: the constructive game. Such people often want an opportunity to use their enterprise, energy and ingenuity. Could this be used in a constructive way?

Information networks in any community quickly identify such people. This identification will be made easier by the naming process that is also part of the positive revolution (and which will be described on page 57). Such a naming process

SELFISH

BLOCKED

will bring about the loss of respect for that person by the local community. All dealings with that person will be on this basis.

The key weapon against selfishness is perception. Quite often the macho, selfish, rip-off person is regarded as a demi-hero. Young men want to impress their peers and the young women around. A gradual change in perception of such people from heroes to social cockroaches is the most powerful way of changing behaviour.

'That's not so smart ... '

'That's not so brave ... '

'That is just plain selfish ... '

Almost everyone needs the respect of other people at some level.

6 EFFECTIVENESS

The basic principle of effectiveness is represented by the thumb of the hand. Because without the thumb, the hand is useless. Whenever we hold tools, a pencil or other things we must use the thumb.

Without effectiveness there is nothing.

The greatest dreams in the world stay as dreams if there is no effectiveness.

Not everyone can be born beautiful or intelligent but everyone can become effective.

Effectiveness is a skill that we can build up for ourselves. We only need the will to do it.

Yet there are very few really effective people. Any employer will employ an effective person ahead of any other person. I, myself, admire effectiveness more than I admire intelligence.

Why is effectiveness so rare? Because we have to build it up until it becomes a habit. Otherwise our laziness and emotions destroy our effectiveness.

What is effectiveness?

Effectiveness is setting out to do something and doing it.

It is as simple as that.

Effectiveness needs three things:

1. CONTROL: you are in control of your own actions and you know what you are trying to do.
2. CONFIDENCE: like a skilled craftsman you are confident that you can do the task.
3. DISCIPLINE: to give patience, perseverance and concentration.

These three things are not going to come about suddenly through an act of will. Like any skill the skill of effectiveness has to be built up gradually through training and practice.

Any task can be divided into very small steps that are easy to take. So you take a small step at a time and complete the task.

In the same way the skill of effectiveness can be built up a small step at a time.

Set yourself small steps and carry them out.

What things are under your control? Being punctual and on time is a very simple thing but excellent training in effectiveness. Make a habit of always being exactly on time. Set yourself

BIG STEPS

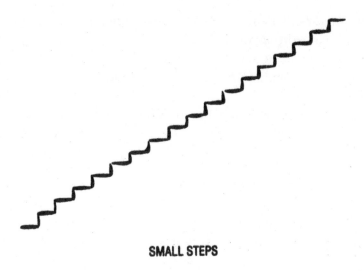

SMALL STEPS

punctuality tasks. Arrange to meet a friend in a distant town at some exact time. See if you can both be there.

Suppose you set out to carve the symbol of the positive revolution, the hand, in stone or wood. Very slowly and very carefully you would work on the carving, a little bit each day. The task is totally under your control. At first you would just carve the outline of the hand in wood or stone. It would not be very good. The next carving would be better. Then you would move on to semi-relief carving with the hand emerging from the wood or stone. Then you might move on to full three-dimensional hands.

Is this a pointless task? No. It is training in the discipline, focus and perseverance of effectiveness. How many carvings should you make? There is no limit.

Effectiveness needs achievement. We like to see what we have done. We get satisfaction from achievement.

An author who writes just 1,000 words a day, every day, will have written five books in a year. Small things add up. But waiting until you are inspired before writing may mean that you never write anything.

So you look at the completed carvings of the hand and you get a sense of improvement and achievement. You give them to friends.

Whenever there is any task to do and you do it, you should pause to say: 'I have done that task and I have done it well.'

The Joy of Effectiveness

What is wonderful about effectiveness is that it becomes a joy and source of happiness. This is based on the following factors:

1. As we get involved in something that thing becomes more interesting. As we get involved with the skill of effectiveness we become more interested in it – in ourselves and in others. Why was I effective here? Why was I not effective there?

2. As we develop the discipline of effectiveness then all tasks get much easier. We can simply decide to do a task and then do it. Instead of battling with our emotions of the moment ('I don't feel like doing it') we just do it. There are no more battles.

3. There is joy in achievement. We look back with pride on what we have done. Over time our achievements build up. We could keep a diary of achievements.

4. As we become more effective we become far more able to set up our own business or far more valuable to an employer. Employers are always looking for effective people.

All these things arise from developing the skill of effectiveness.

That skill of effectiveness will also be used to energize the positive revolution.

The success of Weight Watchers is that people can stand up in front of others and take pride in their achievement of losing weight. In a similar way the joy of effectiveness can become the hobby of achievement. This involves the companionship of working with others, the involvement of designing and planning a task, and the sense of accomplishment in telling others what has been achieved. All these things come together in the idea of the E-Clubs which are set up to provide a way in which 'effectiveness' and achievement can become a hobby. Setting up an E-Club is described in the Appendix (page 119).

Education

Education teaches reading, writing, arithmetic and a lot of knowledge. The reading, writing and arithmetic are basic skills which everyone needs to survive in society – and to contribute.

There is, however, a skill missing from traditional education. This is the skill of thinking. I do not mean thinking in the sense of argument or analysis but thinking in the sense of 'effectiveness'. This is the thinking needed to get things done: objectives, priorities, alternatives, other people's views, creativity, decisions, choices, planning and consequences of action.

We have literacy and numeracy but we need 'operacy' or the skill of doing. Many years ago I designed the CoRT thinking lessons for the deliberate and direct teaching of thinking as a school subject. These lessons are now widely used throughout the world with several countries making them compulsory in all schools. Intelligence is a potential just like the horsepower of a car. To use that potential the driver needs to develop skill. That is the skill of thinking.

Education must teach effectiveness.

Knowledge is not enough. Knowledge without effectiveness can be very dangerous. It can mean that the people with knowledge get into positions of power and do not know how to be effective.

The new education of the positive revolution must teach the thinking skills necessary for effectiveness, leadership and the skills of dealing with other people.

7 SELF-IMPROVEMENT

Suppose we invent a new form of greeting which one person could say to another when they meet. Instead of 'Good morning' or 'Good day' or 'How are you?' we would use this new greeting.

The greeting is: 'Today is a better day.'

This means that whoever you are talking to is one day older than yesterday and as we should be improving with each day we live, then today that person is better than he or she was yesterday.

Of course, some grumpy people would reply that today is not a better day because: he has stomach ache today and did not have it yesterday; because she lost her job today; because it is raining today. But all these things are unimportant if, within yourself, you are better today.

Self-improvement is a day-by-day, slow process. Like the third finger on the hand, self-improvement needs to be there all the time. That is the finger on which we put a wedding ring which usually signals some improvement in our lives.

Self-improvement can take place in any of four directions:

1. Developing positive attitudes, habits and skills. These include things like being constructive, the skill of effectiveness and the habit of contributing.

2. Reducing the domination of bad habits and attitudes such as laziness, selfishness, depression and intolerance.
3. Getting better at whatever it is (work, job, task) that you are doing.
4. Acquiring specific new skills.

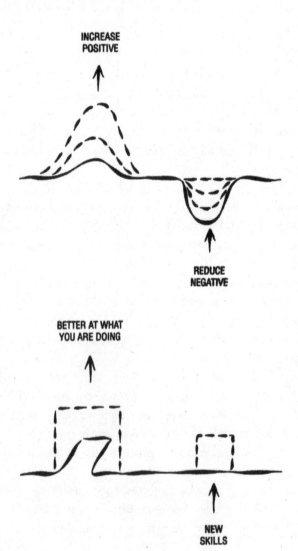

In the USA an increased consciousness of diet and physical fitness, as well as the dangers of smoking and high blood pressure has led to a decline in the rates of heart disease.

Instead of just hoping that tomorrow will be better than today, we can do something today that will make us a little better when we wake up tomorrow than we were yesterday.

Increasing the Positive

The first direction for self-improvement is the beginning, development and improvement of the positive attitudes and habits. The positive attitude that is the basis of the positive revolution.

The constructive attitude which is a way of putting the positive attitude into action. It is also the opposite of the negative and destructive attitude.

The habit of contribution. Seeking for ways to contribute and making contributions in all three areas (self, local, country).

- Practising, and enjoying, the skill of effectiveness.
- Keeping self-improvement in mind.
- Behaving towards other people according to the basic principle of respect.
- Taking an interest in more things. Opening up your mind to new things.
- Becoming more interesting in your conversations and discussions.
- Making an effort to be helpful and agreeable.
- Pausing to assess what you are doing. Praising the good points and noting the weaknesses.

Reducing the Negative

The second direction for improvement is reducing the domination of certain negatives. These are not all going to disappear at once – or ever – but a slight reduction is worth having.

- Making fewer instant judgements. Being less sharp in our emotional reactions.
- Being more tolerant of other people and less critical.
- Being less negative and destructive.
- Being less dogmatic and more willing to listen to other views and alternatives.
- Not taking offence so easily.
- Reducing laziness, sloppiness and unreliability.
- Reducing the amount of time just spent in 'time-filling'.
- Not being so passive.
- Not being so helpless and despairing.
- Not giving up so easily if everything does not work out at once.

Any individual can add to this list his or her own personal areas for improvement.

Some of these will automatically be reduced if we improve the positive aspects already mentioned – which is a more effective way of doing it.

Better At What You Are Doing

Suffering, boredom and time-filling are all negative uses of time – though suffering can sometimes be used in a positive way.

- If you are doing a job, can it be done better? Can the job be done more efficiently or more effectively?

- If you take an interest in the job, does it become more interesting?
- If you have to cook, is it worth trying some new dishes?
- If you have to walk along a certain road, can you notice new things as you walk along?
- If you have to work with some people, can you get to know them better?

If you get to enjoy what you have to do anyway then there is so much more of the day available for enjoyment.

New Skills

Why should we be content with the skills we have? The mother of a friend of mine is learning to play Beethoven piano sonatas that she has never played before.

In learning anything there is first of all a difficult period when it seems too much trouble. But after that period things become easier and more enjoyable:

- Learning a new language.
- Learning to build, decorate or do plumbing.
- Learning to dance.
- Learning to paint pictures or play a musical instrument.
- Learning about a new subject.
- Learning a new sport or a new game.
- Learning to write computer code.
- Learning to be a teacher.
- Learning to provide medical care.
- Starting a new career or profession.
- Setting up a new business.

Involvement and adventure keep the mind young and energetic. Who has drawn the line that says: 'Beyond this point in your life you must not do anything new'?

Emotions

There are some religions which say that emotions are the cause of trouble and suffering in this world so we should seek to suppress or get rid of emotions.

But emotions are the sauce of life. We add sauce to a meal to give it flavour and to make it more enjoyable. So we should enjoy our emotions in the same way. We are not machines.

If, however, you are a slave to your emotions then you can no longer enjoy them. You would not choose to eat only sauce and no meal. You would not choose to make the sauce so hot that you burned your mouth and upset your digestion.

So self-improvement means gaining control of emotions.

Instead of an immediate emotional reaction there is a small pause and then the reaction.

Instead of thinking that things can only be looked at in one way, there is the habit of humour which allows us to switch our way of looking at things. Maybe something is not what we think it is.

Human nature is frightened, insecure, greedy, aggressive, hungry for immediate reward and subject to group pressure. Self-improvement is not going to change human nature but we learn to ride wild horses by understanding their nature and gradually gaining control.

When people are depressed they feel negative. They feel that this depressed state is the real true state of their being. They now regard the times when they were happy as false and artificial. This is a very common feeling. Yet it is a false feeling. It is a feeling we need to turn around the opposite way.

Being depressed is like having a cold. When we are depressed that is the false feeling. When we are depressed that is being unwell. Being positive and happy is the more natural state. So we wait for the depression to pass (and help it pass) rather than sit back in despair.

When you set out to diet and then find yourself eating a big meal you are likely to give up in despair. When you set out on self-improvement and you cannot keep it up, then you are likely to despair and to give it up. This is nonsense. No one is going to be an instant saint every minute of the day. If you are a saint for only one minute a day and eventually you become a saint for two minutes a day that is improvement.

Self-improvement is a gradual process that accepts all manner of ups and downs. But it should start today. Not tomorrow because tomorrow never comes.

8 RESPECT

Respect is symbolized by the second finger on the hand. When you close your fingers together it is obvious that the second finger is longer than all the others. This is to remind you that respect for other people takes precedence over everything else.

Respect and human values go together. We respect the humanity and human values of another person. We respect the individuality of another person. Both are important. It is not much use respecting human values in the abstract and having no respect for individuals. There is no better definition of civilization than respect for others. The Any that insists that self-expression and freedom are more important than consideration for others is less than civilized.

A revolution that forgets about people is no revolution but a retrogression (a step backwards). A revolution that treats people badly in order to do them good is a contradiction. The purpose of any revolution is that the people should benefit – not only ultimately but even while the revolution is going on.

That is why respect is so central to the positive revolution.

Love is wonderful when you can manage it. But love has its doubts, its insecurities, its quarrels, its misunderstandings and its hatreds. It is because love is so wonderful that it is not so suitable for everyday use. Champagne is wonderful but we could not drink it all the time.

It is difficult to love your enemies – even though we should try.

Respect is much more practical than love.

Respect is treating each other person as a human being with the dignity of a human being.

Respect is treating others as you would wish to be treated yourself.

You can say to someone: 'I do not like you but I respect you as a person.'

Historically, the Chinese people didn't have a strong religion. Instead, hundreds of years ago, a scholar called Confucius laid down the rules of how people should treat each other. In contrast to Western religions, Confucius was not interested in the souls of people. He was only interested in how people behaved towards each other in society. He claimed that if everyone behaved properly towards other people civilization would work.

In that one word 'respect' we seek to cover the whole aspect of behaving properly towards other people.

You cannot have a 'high love' and a 'low love' towards someone because love is there or it is not there.

But respect is a scale. You can have a very high respect for someone (for example, a person who contributes a lot). For another person you can have a low respect. This indicates the minimum respect that person deserves as a human being (basic human rights).

Because of this flexibility of respect we can use it in a more practical way. We can always respect someone in our treatment of that person, even if not in our feelings towards that person.

The degree of respect we feel towards someone and the expression of that respect may be at any point along the scale of respect.

The expression of degrees of respect is also a powerful weapon in the way people can affect the behaviour of other people. One person, because of selfishness, might have minimal respect from those around. Another person who contributes a great deal may have very high respect.

So respect works at three levels:

1. Respect is the protection of the basic human rights of any individual.
2. Respect for others is a fundamental principle of the positive revolution and reminds us that people are what matters most in the end.
3. Respect is the way we indicate to people their value in society. Respect is a reward and acknowledgement of their contribution.

Human Dignity and Human Rights

Lack of respect is the most basic crime of all because it covers most other crimes. Murder and torture are the most extreme cases of lack of respect for the lives of others.

It should be said that in the animal kingdom there is often a total lack of respect. One animal kills another animal because it is in the nature of the jaguar or hawk to kill. There is not the slightest consideration of rights. Civilization is civilization because of the concept of respect for basic human rights.

Do human rights mean that society has an obligation to provide you with all the things that you need? This is not quite the same. There is an absolute right to be protected from murder and torture because these are not necessary. Society can only provide health, education, housing and food as far as this is possible.

You may have a bucket that holds five litres but the amount you can put into that bucket depends on the water available. Some resources are limited. There is a great need for new ideas, creative and design thinking, in order to make the best use of limited resources. Some rights can be absolute (freedom from tyranny, torture, oppression, assault) and can be granted by people abstaining from inflicting this behaviour on others. Other rights are limited by resources (health, food, education).

It is possible to be poor and to retain human dignity and human rights. A very large part of the population of the world is poor. The way out of poverty is through the creation and distribution of wealth, through self-help, and through the positive and constructive attitudes of the positive revolution. History has shown that the exercise of rights does not itself create resources.

METHODS

We have looked at the five fundamental principles of the positive revolution, now we need to look at the methods. How will the principles be put into action? How will the principles bring about change?

1. PERCEPTION: Instead of the logic and dogma of ideology there is the immense power of human perception to create and change values.

    On page 91 we will look at the power of the positive revolution and that arises from both principles and methods.

2. NAMING: Through the development of a new vocabulary we can assign the new values in society so as to encourage the constructive and contributing behaviour of the positive revolution.

3. SYMBOLS: Visible symbols and signals which spread the message of the positive revolution give a sense of belonging and reinforce the attitudes.

4. ORGANIZATION: The positive revolution is not centralized but is based on the work of individuals and groups.

5. EDUCATION: The need for a simple new education that covers the basic needs of people but also instructs in thinking and effectiveness.

6. THINKING: The use of creativity and practical thinking to design the constructive steps that can be taken towards a better society. Not argument or criticism.

It will be seen that the methods of the positive revolution are very different from the methods of traditional revolutions. For example:

- There are no enemies.
- Everyone can take part.
- The benefits start immediately and not only after the revolution has succeeded.
- There are no leaders.

9 PERCEPTION

- Beware of people who give passionate speeches.
- Beware of people who shout.
- Beware of people who use a lot of emotional adjectives.
- Beware of people who show you your enemies.

Such people want to cook your perceptions in exactly the same way as a cook fries chips in a pan. The cook is in control.

- Perception is more powerful than logic.
- Perception is more powerful than emotions.
- Perception is more powerful than belief.

Perception is not in the eyes or ears but it is what the brain does with the information that comes from the eyes and ears (and other senses). Perception is the sense that the brain makes from this input. It is this sense that determines how we see the world.

Crude Perceptions

It is getting dark and you see the shape of a man in your house – but you cannot see his face clearly. You may be frightened because you think it might be an intruder. When you see the person clearly you see that he is: a member of your family, a friend, a person you know but dislike, a stranger. Your emotions will follow identification or perception.

In this example we identify the man by his face. At other times we identify things by the label attached to them, for example, packaged food in the supermarket.

In our language and our thinking we have built up labels that are very simple and crude:

- Us/them
- Friend/enemy
- Hero/villain

These labels make us perceive things in these crude ways and our emotions follow. If someone is an enemy then we hate that person. That is why traditional revolutions have had to label enemies and why they have needed to cook perceptions.

We are trapped within the traditional perceptions that are available to us through culture and language. The positive revolution has to find a way of getting us out of this trap.

We might look at capitalists and say that some capitalists have been greedy and have exploited people. This may have been true in the past and is probably true in some cases today. So capitalists are 'enemies'. Therefore we must hate all capitalists and seek to destroy capitalism. We do not have any better method of creating wealth but that does not matter because enemies must be destroyed.

Or we might look at those who fight for better human rights and perhaps a more fair distribution of wealth and we say they must be 'socialist' and therefore they are enemies. Since they are enemies we must oppose them and resist all their demands.

It is obvious that simple fixed perceptions do not allow us to be constructive. They may be necessary for the traditional

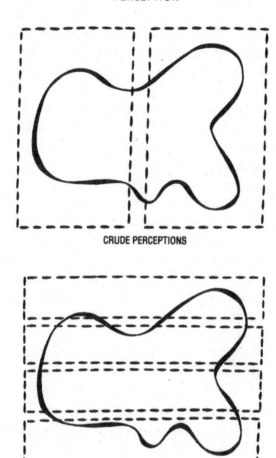

CRUDE PERCEPTIONS

NEW PERCEPTIONS

destructive revolution but not for the positive constructive revolution.

But instead of fixed perceptions we need ways of changing perceptions. We need tools to enable us to see things in a different way.

It is the role of the positive revolution to provide such tools. These tools include the following:

1. **HUMOUR:** This is the best protection against dogma, arrogance, righteousness – and also despair. A sense of humour always keeps in mind the possibility of seeing things in another way.
2. **NAMING:** Instead of being forced to use the crude labels that have been provided by culture and tradition we can invent some new and better labels in order to guide our perceptions in a more positive way and to allow us to escape from the tyranny of the old labels.
3. **ALTERNATIVES:** The simple habit of saying to yourself in any situation or any conversation: 'There is at least one other way to look at this.' You may never find this other way but you are sure of the possibility.
4. **THINKING:** The thinking lessons that we have taught in schools are specifically designed to train people to be able to broaden and change perceptions. These will be discussed later (page 81).
5. **INFORMATION:** By itself information does not change perceptions or create new ones. But information can strengthen or weaken perceptions. So when we set out to build new perceptions information can give substance to the new perceptions. Information can also spread the new perceptions.

Traditional revolutions are about dogma and organization; the positive revolution is about people and perception.

- People must be able to change perceptions.
- People must have a wider range of perceptions from which to choose.
- People should not be locked rigidly into one fixed set of perceptions.

Humour

No serious revolution has ever put humour as one of its key methods.

This is because traditional revolutions are based on ideology, dogma, certainty, righteousness and solemnity.

This is because traditional revolutions are based on the crude perceptions of 'friend' and 'enemy' and the necessary hatred. Humour could threaten this polarization.

Humour is one of the very few ways we have of changing perception. In humour we switch, suddenly, from looking at things in one way to looking at them in another. A person telling a joke leads us along a path and then, suddenly, we see the crazy logic of the joke.

Humour tells us that the mind works in patterns but that it is possible to switch the patterns.

Art and culture and tradition have always given us ready-made perceptions: 'This is the way you must look at things', 'These are the perceptions you must use.' This can be valuable but it can also be dangerous.

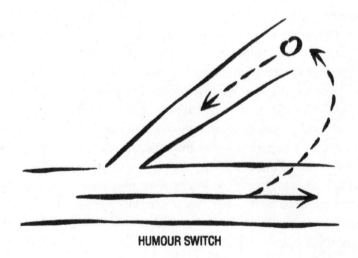

HUMOUR SWITCH

Information

Information does not form perceptions because information is organized according to existing perceptions. Information feeds perceptions. Information allows us to choose which perception to use.

Because the positive revolution does not have a central organization, information is extremely important so that all the people who are part of the revolution can know what is going on.

Technology has provided us with formal media networks like the internet, radio and television. It has also made information more widely accessible.

This information technology allows us to build the concept of the positive revolution. Marxism arose from the industrial revolution. The positive revolution arises from the information revolution.

The media – both in the traditional sense and online – can spread the concepts of the positive revolution either passively or actively.

The media comments on what is happening in society. Journalists, bloggers and other online commentators can pick up and use some of the new concepts and 'names' that are part of the positive revolution.

In a more active sense the media can become a central factor in spreading the positive revolution. The principles of 'contribution', 'constructive' and 'effective' can be amplified directly by writers as part of their ordinary work and also as a basis for special programmes (for example, reviews of instances of constructive effort and contribution).

Not all writers will be happy with the positive revolution. Some prefer to be negative. Some can only exercise their talent in being critical and destructive. They still believe, following traditional beliefs, that this is the way to get a better society.

On the one hand there is the formal, traditional media (television, radio, print) and on the other there is the informal media which includes social media, word-of-mouth communication in local communities, communication at the place of work and communication in any conversation.

This informal communication is extremely important. Those people who become identified as the 'communicators' in a community have a valued role to play.

The symbols and new 'names' of the positive revolution will help this informal communication network by providing substance for the communication. For example, the extent of someone's contribution is easier to communicate than just a feeling that he is a good person.

10 NAMING

There are thousands of plants and each one has a different name.

A doctor can recognize dozens of different diseases and give a name to each.

Because language is quite capable of describing behaviour after it has happened we have not developed the habit of giving names to different types of behaviour. Because we do not have these names our perceptions are very limited.

For example, we might say we 'like' someone or 'love' someone or 'dislike' or 'hate'. These are very simple and crude terms.

The Inuit in the cold north spend the dark winter months very close to each other in their igloos. Because they are so close they have developed about 20 different ways of saying 'I like you'. For example there is one word to say: 'I like you very much but I would not want to go seal-hunting with you.'

In order to operate the values of the positive revolution we need to create new names so that we can see things differently. Without such names we may be able to describe things but not see them that way.

People

In order to make concrete the values of the positive revolution we need to name categories of behaviour. Once we have these named categories we can talk about them and think about them.

We can identify nine categories of behaviour. People who show a certain type of behaviour can be perceived as being in one of these categories. There are four positive, four negative, and one neutral category:

CATEGORY ONE: Behaviour that is constructive and also very effective. The effective part is very important. A person who is a leader and organizer. Taken all together this is a person who can make things happen in a positive and constructive way. Because of these qualities this is a person who contributes. If a person has all these qualities but is not in a position to contribute at this moment, we might say 'potential category one'.

CATEGORY TWO: This is a person who is actually contributing a great deal at this moment. Such a person may have none of the qualities of category one but nevertheless is contributing. For example, a rich man who has inherited money may give a lot of money to help the poor. A talented artist may use his or her talents to contribute to society. A famous sports star may use his or her talents to contribute. The contribution is great but the qualities of category one are not present.

CATEGORY THREE: This is someone who is hardworking, cooperative, helpful and also effective. The difference between category one and category three is that in category one there are also the qualities of leadership, organizing ability and constructive initiative. Someone in category three might be very good in a project team or when the task has been defined for him or her.

58

CATEGORY FOUR: This person is positive, agreeable, pleasant and cheerful. This person does the job he or she is doing just well enough. This person is nice to have around but is not very effective.

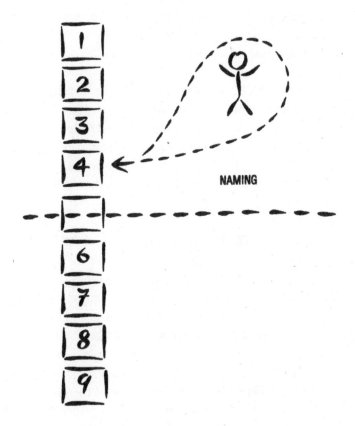

CATEGORY FIVE: Behaviour that is neutral, behaviour that is passive. You cannot say anything positive about this person but you cannot say anything negative either. A person who is apathetic and content to drift from moment to moment with no sense of involvement and no sense of control over destiny. This is the neutral category.

CATEGORY SIX: This behaviour is critical, negative and destructive. The person may be highly intelligent but uses that intelligence not to build but to destroy. In a group this person does not make proposals but attacks the proposals of others. In attitude this person may be gloomy or depressed or may not. Some negative people enjoy being negative so much that they are not gloomy. Category six people still believe that negativity is the best way towards progress.

CATEGORY SEVEN: Behaviour that is totally selfish. Behaviour that is exploitative or corrupt. There is a wide range of behaviour from simple selfishness to extreme corruption. This person is not seeking to hurt others and may be within the law. The characteristic of category seven behaviour is that it is totally selfish. Category seven behaviour is the exact opposite of contribution.

CATEGORY EIGHT: This is the behaviour of the bully. This is the behaviour of the person who seeks to get what he or she wants by demanding it from others. The category eight person uses force to get his or her own way. Both category seven and category eight people may be exploiters but in the case of category eight it is a deliberate exploitation of other people and the use of force to achieve that.

CATEGORY NINE: This is the behaviour of the outlaw. This is the behaviour of the person who has no respect at all for other people or the rights of other people. This is the criminal who has no conscience and no morals. This is the sort of person who would murder for a small sum of money. Note that category eight people may acknowledge the rights of others but are capable of infringing those rights from time to time. Category nine people acknowledge no rights at all except their own intentions.

In time there may arise a name for each category. For example, the behaviour of category seven is parasitic so we might call such people 'cockroaches'. The behaviour of category six is to draw their energy from others so we might call them 'ticks' or 'leeches' that live on the blood they suck.

There could be competitions for people to find the best names for these categories. We can use the categories right away without special names:

'He's a category four person. He is nice enough but he won't get anything done.'

'He is not really category one. He does contribute but that is because of his position, not his constructive energy. He is more category two – but that is very valuable.'

'I have heard that he is definitely category seven so we shall have to keep an eye on him.'

'You would not think so to look at her, she is so small and frail, but she is definitely category one.'

'We need to find a lot more category three people in order to get this project moving. We are not short of ideas but we need action.'

'Don't invite her – she is pure category six.'

Once the categories are there we can use them to praise and reward behaviour. We can use them to encourage behaviour because if someone knows that he or she is regarded as being in a certain category then that person will try to live up to a good image.

We can use the categories to blame people and to point out to them their failings. We can use the categories to let people know what other people feel about them. We can use the categories to encourage people to try to move upwards out of the category in which they are placed. In moving upwards you do not have to move only to the category above.

For example, a category six person could jump to category three immediately.

The categories provide a language in which the members of the positive revolution can value the behaviour of other people.

It is important to make clear that the person is not locked into the category forever. These are categories of *behaviour,* not of character.

So we should really say: 'You behave like a category six person.'

There is always the option of change.

If a person shows no inclination to change then we perceive that person as within his or her category and treat that person accordingly.

By virtue of their positions, teachers, doctors and journalists could be category one or two people because they are in a position to make significant contributions. But a teacher may be category four or even category five. Many journalists are category six.

The heroes and villains of the positive revolution are defined according to the values of the categories. So people who are selfish are villains. People who are constructive and effective are heroes.

The vices and virtues of the positive revolution are also defined by the categories taken together with the basic principles. Being negative is a vice, so is being passive and apathetic (even though this is neutral on the category list). Being effective is a virtue. Being positive is a virtue but not as high a virtue as being positive and also effective.

A person need not be entirely within a category. For example, you might say: 'Sometimes he shows category eight behaviour.' In this way the categories also become adjectives.

Could there be more categories? Yes, and in time there may be. For the moment it is enough to become familiar with nine.

Situations

There is a need for new words to describe particular situations so that we can perceive these situations more easily and refer to them more readily. The examples given here are only an indication of what is needed.

'I don't like you and you don't like me and we disagree on most things but it is in both our interests that we work together effectively on this matter.'

We need a single word to cover the pragmatism of this arrangement. We need a word to bridge the friend/enemy division given us by normal perception and language. In English we might just say 'frenemy' by combining friend and enemy.

'In this situation any sensible politician would have to make these necessary public noises. They do not mean anything but are full of the right sounds.'

We need a single word which acknowledges the necessity for certain political noises. Such a word would make it easier to distinguish between serious political statements and routine noise. We might say 'n.p.n.' for necessary public noises.

'Knowing what to do is not enough. There is a skill in designing how something can be done and in carrying it out. There is a skill in making something happen.' Some time ago I invented the word 'operacy' to cover the specific skill of doing.

11 SYMBOLS

Why does a revolution need symbols?

- To allow the revolution to spread. The symbols are a signal to those who do not yet belong to join. You see a signal and you are curious as to its meaning so you inquire and learn about the positive revolution.
- To give a sense of belonging and identity to those who already belong to the positive revolution. You can recognize and greet fellow members. You can see that you are not alone in the revolution.
- To remind those taking part of the principles of positive revolution. To reinforce the aims and intentions of the positive revolution.
- To provide a way for any member of the revolution to make a very small contribution. The minimal contribution – even if you do nothing else – would be to display or wear a symbol.
- To provide a basis for power. If you see the symbols all around you then you know that the revolution has a lot of support. This is important in a democracy because support means votes.

Yellow

Yellow is the colour of the positive revolution. Yellow represents sunlight, brightness, hope and being positive. The sun rises each day and creates a new day. The sun provides the ultimate energy for the world. Yellow is cheerful. Yellow emphasizes the positive nature of the revolution. A traditional revolutionary colour is red but red represents death and destruction and that is the opposite of the positive revolution.

Yellow Book

This is the 'yellow book' and can be referred to as such.

> 'Have you read the yellow book?'
> 'Do you agree with the yellow book?'
> 'Read the yellow book again.'

Because there is no central organization to the positive revolution the yellow book is the handbook and serves to coordinate the attitudes and thinking of the members of the positive revolution. The yellow book is both the handbook and the reference manual. Every machine has an instruction manual. The yellow book is the manual for the positive revolution. That is why it is so short.

Yellow Hand

The open hand with the fingers spread out is the symbol of the positive revolution.

The hand represents the five fundamental principles of the positive revolution:

1. Thumb: means effectiveness.
2. Index finger: points in the constructive direction.
3. Second finger: respect, which includes human values.
4. Third finger: self-improvement – getting better every day.
5. Little finger: contribution – no matter how small.

The open hand does not have to be yellow but if there is to be a colour then this should be yellow.

The hand also represents 'doing'. This term of 'doing' involves both thinking and work.

The hand reminds us that the positive revolution is not just a revolution of philosophy but of constructiveness, of effectiveness and of contribution. The heroes are people who make things happen. The hand is what has enabled mankind to make things happen.

Yellow Armband

This is a very important symbol of the positive revolution because it is so visible and makes the revolution visible to everyone else.

The yellow armband may be made of cloth or a strip of plastic. It is one-inch wide and is worn on the wrist or on the arm just above the elbow. Where this is not convenient the armband may be worn as a wristband or in any other place, for example, protruding from a pocket.

Members of the positive revolution are not obliged to wear the yellow armband but it is an opportunity to express to themselves and to others their agreement with the principles of the positive revolution.

Three Circles

As a graphic design the three circles of concern is also a symbol of the positive revolution. This type of symbol is more of a reminder to those who are already part of the revolution that they should seek to contribute in the three areas. For example, this could be a symbol at meetings rather than a public symbol.

1. Circle 1: Self and self-improvement.
2. Circle 2: Family, friends, local community and work community.
3. Circle 3: The country and the world.

Greeting

There is the suggested greeting which is:
'Today is a better day.'

This is used by people as they greet each other or pass in the street. It emphasizes the positive attitude, the willingness to work to make things better and the steady progress of self-improvement.

There may be many reasons why today is not actually better (economics, rain, quarrels, ill health) but the greeting reminds everyone that internally each person can be better each day.

Salute

This is very simple. The hand is raised with the fingers spread as if you were showing someone the number five. Usually the hand would not be raised higher than the face.

The salute is intended as a casual greeting. It is certainly not a militant salute.

Slogan

The positive revolution does not have a dogma or an ideology so there is no magic in a slogan.

The slogan, therefore, repeats the three key attitudes of the positive revolution:
'Positive, constructive, your contribution.'

Name

The revolution is most simply called:

'The positive revolution.'

In time the revolution may come to be called 'the yellow revolution', but at first that would not be as easily understood as 'the positive revolution'.

The name for those taking part in the positive revolution will develop by itself over time. Two names that would seem appropriate to me are 'the constructors' and 'the quiet ones'.

The name 'the constructors' indicates very clearly the constructive nature of the positive revolution. Change is going to come about through building and not through destroying.

The name 'the quiet ones' indicates that change will come through steady and effective contribution, not through shouting and demonstration.

Flag

The positive revolution does not need a flag since it is a quiet revolution. But in order to prevent the emergence of a flag that might give the wrong impression, there is a design for a flag.

The flag is a simple yellow flag with a pink heart in the top corner near the flagpole.

The yellow is the positive colour of the revolution.

The pink heart symbolizes humanity and human values.

FLAG

12 ORGANIZATION

The positive revolution is a revolution of people and perception, not of central organization and dogma.

The grass that spreads over the land, the trees that create a forest, are not directed by a central organization. They spread because each blade of grass and each tree is a living thing with the power of spreading. There are seeds which spread and from each seed grows the plant.

In the same way the positive revolution is a self-organizing system which is made up of the people who belong.

Every member of the positive revolution belongs first as an individual. This is an individual who in heart and mind agrees with the principles of the positive revolution.

Members of the Positive Revolution

Everyone can be a member.

There is no membership fee, no test and no certification.

You belong if you want to belong.

But the positive revolution is a revolution of action and doing. It is not just a matter of agreeing or believing in the principles. That is only the first step.

In practice you only really belong to the revolution when you contribute your effectiveness and your constructive action.

Membership of the positive revolution is at first a contract with yourself. How do you prove to yourself that you are taking part in the positive revolution in an active way? There is self-improvement. There is constructive contribution. If you are not 'doing' anything then you do not really belong to the positive revolution.

You do not have to join a group but if you join a group then the members of your group will make clear to you whether you belong to the positive revolution or not.

With some movements you belong if you pay. With some movements you belong if you believe. With the positive revolution you belong if you 'do' (action).

You can keep your membership silently in your heart. It may be that you do not want others to know. It may be that you are in a position where you must be neutral (like a judge). You can belong silently to the positive revolution.

You may want to show your membership to those around you. You can do this by wearing the yellow armband, by using the greeting or salute. You can show your membership by talking about the positive revolution or about this yellow book.

You should be proud of belonging to the positive revolution. That is why you want to show others that you belong. If you show others then the others can see that you are interested in the positive revolution and you can be invited to join a group.

By showing in a visible way that you are part of the positive revolution you also help the revolution to spread. As this happens you can look around and see that you now belong to a large group of people who are part of the revolution.

You can be part of the positive revolution at every minute of the day (which is the best) or you can switch into your revolutionary role for certain periods only.

Groups

Individual members of the positive revolution will soon form themselves into groups. There may be groups in the local community, at work, amongst friends. The following types of groups can emerge:

COMMUNITY CIRCLES: A group that forms to tackle in a constructive way the problems of the community. There may be several such circles in any community.

QUALITY CIRCLES: A group that forms at work in order to see how the work process can be improved. This group wants to contribute constructively to what is going on at work.

PROJECT CIRCLES: This is a group that collects together with the specific purpose of carrying through a particular project (a building, an irrigation scheme, etc.). All the energies of the group are directed, constructively, towards this purpose.

CONCERN CIRCLES: These are groups that form because all the members of the group have a particular concern. This concern might be something like local pollution or a high local crime rate.

YELLOW CIRCLES: These are groups formed by people who are committed to the positive revolution and come together as a group to see how the positive revolution can be put into action. Their 'project' and their 'concern' are the positive revolution itself.

E-CLUBS: These clubs are not strictly part of the positive revolution but are designed to build up the habits of effectiveness and achievement that are so important for the positive

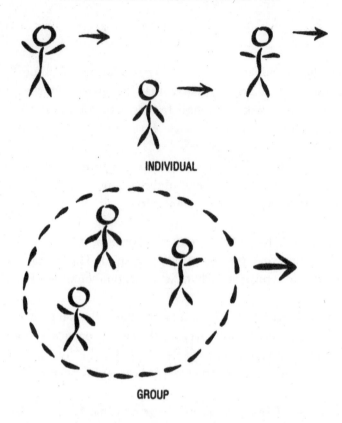

INDIVIDUAL

GROUP

revolution. Members of an E-Club can belong to any of the other circles at the same time.

All these circles become like 'new families' to the members of the circle. The circles are part of the 'second circle' of concern (family, friends, local community, workplace).

The working rules of the circles are very simple:

1. The circles embody the five fundamental principles of the positive revolution. Therefore they must be positive and constructive. They must keep clearly in mind the principle of 'respect' and human values. Above all, the members are there to contribute.

2. This yellow book is the reference book for the behaviour of the circles. Nothing may be done in the name of the positive revolution which is not within this yellow book. For example, destructive behaviour, violent behaviour, illegal and criminal activities are specifically excluded. Beware of groups that set up to follow the principles of the positive revolution and then drift away from the fundamental principles to pursue their own ends.

3. The circles are action circles and not just argument or philosophy groups. The emphasis is on the design of constructive action and the carrying through effectively of that action – through the contribution of the members of the circle.

4. The only grounds for expelling a member from a circle are directly destructive behaviour. If the majority decide that this matter is proved then the member must leave. At any time, however, a group may dissolve and re-form leaving out those members which the members of the new group do not want to include. The identity of the old group must end. Assets of the old group must be shared and used constructively.

What might happen in these circles?

There is going to be discussion. The discussion must always be positive and constructive. There is no place for typical critical arguments and disputes over who is right and who is wrong.

There should be a very clear focus on what is being discussed and also on the constructive direction that is to be taken.

The specific purpose of the circles is contribution.

- Where can a contribution be made?
- How can that contribution be carried out effectively?

A circle may devote several meetings simply to listing areas of possible contribution.

There is an emphasis on 'design of action' so that the energy of the circle may be used in the most effective way. Such design may involve creativity and new ideas. The action should always be constructive.

Education Groups

Education is one of the key areas of possible contribution by members of the positive revolution. This area will be discussed separately, in its own right.

Circles may be set up specifically to coordinate and carry out educational work. This may be the sole function of that particular circle.

Education is an ideal form of contribution. Everyone can have something to teach or ways of helping people learn. Education requires only time and effort. Education makes a serious long-term contribution.

Apart from the specific education groups that might be set up, this education aspect might be an important feature of any circle.

Together with this education function we might also put 'information', because information is a type of education.

As a contribution a circle might collect information, sort it out and find ways of making it available to others.

Advice in specific matters is also a type of education and a valuable contribution.

13 SPREAD

The more people that join the positive revolution the more effective it will be. So spread is important.

The positive revolution can spread through people reading this yellow book. They may buy the book or borrow it, read it online or be given it by a friend. So giving the book to people who might be interested is a basic form of spread.

There is word-of-mouth and talk about the positive revolution (and the yellow book) amongst friends and acquaintances.

The media can be involved by discussing the nature of the positive revolution and the principles involved. Some of the media might take a category six attitude but there will be some who recognize the value of the positive attitudes of the revolution.

The visible symbols such as armbands, greetings and salutes will make people curious and they will want to know what is happening.

Interested people may be invited to circle meetings.

The new naming of the positive revolution will gradually spread and people will want to know where it is coming from. For example, reference to someone as 'category three' will arouse curiosity.

Most important of all, the action example of the members of the positive revolution should encourage others to join.

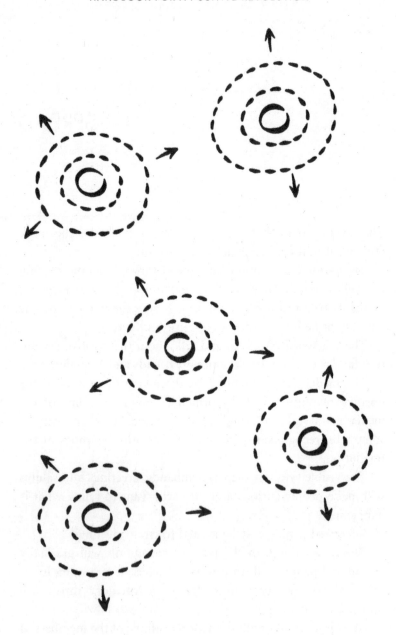

Enemies

The positive revolution has no class of enemies.

Unlike traditional revolutions there is no definition of a group of people or a part of society that can be classed as an enemy and must be hated.

The positive revolution is working towards a better society through the application of attitudes that are positive and constructive and efforts that are effective. These things are going to be energized by the contribution of the members of the revolution.

If groups choose to regard themselves as enemies of the positive revolution then that is their choice. The positive revolution will not respond by classifying them as enemies but will regard them as suffering from temporarily faulty perceptions.

Although there is no class of enemies as such, the value and esteem accorded to individuals will depend on their constructive behaviour and contribution.

The behaviour of a particular individual may place that individual in a low category (say, category seven or eight). That is a judgement on the behaviour of an individual.

Uniformity

Because there is no central organization and no dogma, because individuals can join the revolution as they wish, because individuals can come together to form circles, there is a danger of lack of uniformity.

Although everyone may start out with the right feelings there can be a drift over time so that eventually individuals or groups come to use the cloak of the positive revolution to pursue their old destructive habits. This may happen consciously or unconsciously. It is very important for any member of the revolution to be on guard against this.

People who are not behaving according to the positive principles of the revolution are not part of that revolution – whatever they may claim.

The source of uniformity is this yellow book. It is important that members of the positive revolution remind themselves, and their groups, of its contents from time to time.

14 EDUCATION

Self-improvement is one of the five basic principles of the positive revolution (the third finger).

You can improve through your own efforts or with the help of others.

Education is a key part of the method of the positive revolution.

Education is also a major opportunity area for contribution. Those who say they cannot see how they can contribute should look to the area of education.

Everyone can teach something. Even if this is not true you can help someone to learn. Education does not require physical strength, exceptional talent, money or political power. Education requires time, effort and perseverance. That is why it is so ideal a form of contribution.

For example, as a contribution a yellow circle could set out to teach people how to teach people to teach. The multiplying effect of this activity would be enormous. For every 20 people taught in this way there would be 400 teachers and 8,000 students.

But what should be taught?

The New Education

Traditional education has many years in which to accomplish its task. Even if it does its task well, this takes a long time. Perhaps the important things could be done in a much shorter time so making it more practical to impart education.

In fact traditional education does not do a complete job. For example, the emphasis is on information analysis and argument. There is a need for attention to thinking skills directly. There is a need for attention to the skills of doing. There is a need for attention to the skills of construction rather than just criticism.

So the 'new education' will seek to simplify the curriculum, to make it more practical – and also to enlarge its scope.

The new education is a basic education. It would consist of the following elements:

READING AND WRITING: These are the key tools of further learning and of communication. The best methods of teaching and writing must be chosen, or new methods developed.

MATHEMATICS: This would cover only the basic mathematics needed in ordinary life. Such things would be taught effectively. In traditional education too much mathematics is taught and the result is confusion.

BASIC THINKING SKILLS: These thinking skills would be concerned with perception (broadening and changing), with practical action (doing) and with dealing with other people. They would be based on the successful CoRT method which has many years of experience with millions of students around the world.

THE WORLD AROUND: A basic understanding of the local world around. This would include the institutions, the mechanisms and the basic channels for getting things done.

LEADERSHIP AND EFFECTIVENESS: The specific development of the qualities of personality and behaviour that are so important if people are going to be constructive and are going to be able to contribute.

SPECIFIC SKILLS: To the five core subjects already listed would be added specific skills that were related to a particular area. For example, in the countryside there would be the fundamentals of agriculture. In the city there might be business skills.

LEARNING SKILLS: Here the emphasis would be on the skills required for further learning for those students who are ambitious or talented and want to continue their education further.

Leadership and Effectiveness

Traditional education has focused on academic subjects because the original aim of education was to prepare a few people for special professions (church, law, medicine) which required a large amount of basic knowledge.

But society also required leaders and constructive people.

Individuals also need to learn the habits of effectiveness in order to make full use of their talents and opportunities and in order to be able to contribute.

So education must make a serious effort to train and develop these abilities. This will require new methods and new programmes which can be developed and used by the yellow circles:

- The ability to work in a team.
- The ability to work constructively.
- The ability to design and plan a task.

- The ability to take initiatives.
- The discipline of perseverance and effectiveness.

These are all extremely important.

Such things cannot just be learned from textbooks. People need to be involved in project work. They need to take responsibility for projects.

In this way the learning process also becomes a direct contribution to society since the project itself will have value.

People will need to be trained to look after this type of project training.

Self-help

Self-help is a combination of attitudes, expectations, skills, organization and knowledge.

The attitude is the opposite of passive acceptance and the hope that someone will do everything for you. The attitude is one of setting out to do something for yourself and your community even if the steps are very small at first.

People are always limited by their expectations. If you have no destination, how can you get there? People feel that there are limits and boundaries and that some things are not for them. Such limits are self-imposed. The most powerful source of change is to remove these boundaries in order to open up ambition.

Then there are the skills of thinking and doing. There are skills of 'operacy' (making things happen). There is a basic constructive attitude on which is built a sense of the practical and the creativity of design: 'How can this be done?' The discipline of effectiveness then ensures that something is done thoroughly and done completely.

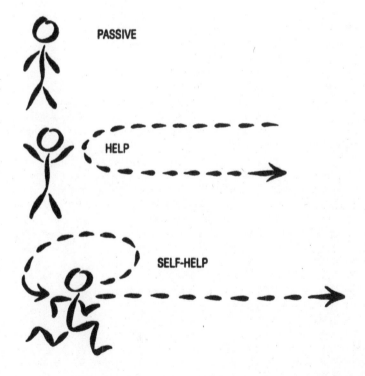

There is a need for the organization of time, of other people, of supplies and of help. Cooperation needs to be organized.

Knowing where to get knowledge and how to make the best use of knowledge is part of the self-help skill. Realizing that there might be a need for new knowledge is also vital.

A 'self-help' programme could be taught as part of the 'new education' or taught as a programme on its own.

15 THINKING

'Thinking' is the final method of the positive revolution.

Members of the positive revolution are not just dedicated hard workers. They are also thinkers. You can push hard against a wall and nothing happens no matter how hard you push. You can dismantle the wall brick by brick.

Thinking is needed to make the maximum use of energy. Thinking is needed for the design of constructive action. Thinking is needed for the creative solution to problems. Thinking is needed to design projects. Thinking is needed to find and define areas of contribution.

Now the thinking that is needed for the positive revolution is very different from traditional thinking. It is not the thinking of attack, criticism, argument and clash. It is not the normal thinking of lawyers and some politicians. It is not the thinking of those who point out the faults in society (though this may be a valuable role).

We need to develop and practise the specific skills of constructive thinking. The circle may need to spend time practising these skills directly in order to become better at such thinking. This could be done using the CoRT thinking programme that has already been mentioned (page 82). A short period of such practice could be part of every circle meeting.

The Six Thinking Hats

This is a very simple and very practical technique for introducing the habits of constructive thinking. It is a sort of role-playing.

There are six hats of different colours and the thinker imagines that he or she is putting on a certain hat or taking off that hat. The hats are as follows:

WHITE HAT: This covers information, data and facts. When you ask for 'white hat thinking' you want only the information – not ideas or arguments.

RED HAT: This covers emotions, feelings and intuitions. Under the red hat the thinker can put forward his or her direct feelings on the subject without any need to justify or explain these feelings. 'Wearing my red hat I think this is a terrible project.'

BLACK HAT: This is the hat of caution and judgement. With the black hat we look at the dangers and difficulties and why something may not work.

YELLOW HAT: This is the hat of optimism. This is the positive hat. Why something will work. What the benefits will be. How something can be done.

GREEN HAT: This is the creative hat. New ideas and alternatives. Proposals and provocations. The green colour suggests the energy of vegetation and growth.

BLUE HAT: This is the overview of process control hat. With the blue hat we stand back and look at our thinking on the subject. With the blue hat we determine what sort of thinking we might do next. With the blue hat we decide which hat to wear next. The blue hat can also be used for summarizing where the thinking has got to at this moment.

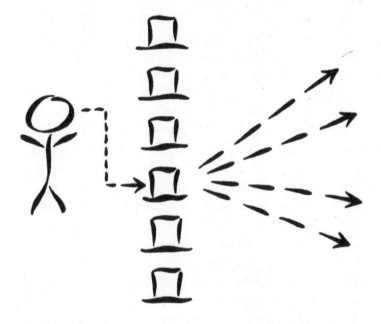

In a discussion you can ask someone to put on a hat or to take off a hat. For example, if someone is being very negative you might say: 'That is great black hat thinking, now I want you to try the yellow hat.'

You can ask the whole group to put on a hat: 'I want everyone here to put on their green hats for four minutes and come up with some new approaches to this problem.'

You can also say that you yourself are putting on a hat: 'Putting on my red hat I'm thinking this is a wonderful idea', or, 'Putting on my black hat I want to point out that this project could be very expensive because printing costs are high.'

In order to explore a subject thoroughly you can set out in advance a programme listing which hat in turn is to be used: 'We shall start with the white hat for the information, then the green hat for some approaches to the matter, then the yellow hat followed by the black hat on each approach, and finally the red hat to see what we now feel.'

It is not enough to be intelligent. Many highly intelligent people are poor thinkers. For example they might just use their intelligence to defend their point of view instead of exploring the subject. They might use their intelligence to destroy instead of to construct.

Intelligence is like the horsepower of a car. It is only a potential. Thinking skill is like driving skill. We have to learn how to drive and we have to learn how to think constructively. There may be powerful cars that are driven badly. There may be highly intelligent minds that are used ineffectively.

So the will and attitude of the revolution (positive and constructive) need to be supplemented by the thinking that can design powerful contributions. Then those designs can be put into action with the discipline and habits of effectiveness. It is in this way that everything comes together for the improvement of society and the benefit of the people in it.

The old thinking is not constructive enough. We need new thinking.

POWER

Where is the power of the positive revolution to come from?

Traditional revolutions use the power of guns, bullets and bombs to achieve their goal. What power is the positive revolution going to use?

The positive revolution will have the following sources of power:

- The power of a positive and constructive attitude.
- The power of the best people.
- The power of perception.
- The power of thinking and of information.
- The power of coordination and alignment.
- The power of support.
- The power of spreading.

The Power of Positive and Constructive Attitudes

A positive attitude gives energy. A constructive attitude can make things happen.

When these two attitudes are placed against the two attitudes of apathy or negativity it is clear that the positive and constructive attitude is going to get more done.

If you have a more powerful engine in your car then you are going to outperform other cars (provided your driving is also good).

So personal power and also social power will arise directly from these attitudes.

A negative attitude says that something cannot be done.

An apathetic attitude says that there is nothing which can be done.

The constructive attitude sets out to find a way of doing it and then does it.

If you know any constructive and positive people you will know that these attitudes give the power of action.

The Power of the Best People

The positive revolution sets out to make the best people.

This is through the emphasis on self-improvement (fourth basic principle) and on education.

This is through the emphasis on effectiveness and on contribution.

This is through the emphasis on thinking, design and creativity.

This is through the emphasis on respect and human values (third basic principle).

In time these excellent people will succeed through their effectiveness and constructive attitude. They will be successful in business and at community level. They will enter established institutions and government because they are obviously the most effective people. In all these positions they will be able to exert the power of these positions.

These people do not have enemies and do not make enemies. They are willing to work with anyone who also has a constructive attitude towards the improvement of society.

THE BEST PEOPLE

It is also likely that many of the best people already in positions of power will see the merit of the positive revolution and its constructive attitude and will want to become members, visibly or in their hearts.

The Power of Perception

The power of perception is not very obvious. The power of perception is subtle and slow but it is very strong.

The power of perception is the power to change values and to set up values. The naming of the 'categories' establishes a value system that can be applied to any individual. This value system can now affect the way people around regard and treat that person. This makes possible peer pressure or group pressure and this is one of the most powerful ways of changing behaviour.

The values and attitudes of the positive revolution can be taken up in the media (television, radio, online, press) and so become part of the culture of society. For example, we might no longer look at critical or negative people with the esteem we now use.

When we have new words for things like 'game-playing' and 'necessary political noises' then there is a clearer perception of what is going on – and this affects the behaviour of people.

An increase in perceptual skill means that people are not going to be so easily fooled by emotion, passion, adjectives, enemies and slogans. The power of hatred becomes diminished.

Then there is the power of humour and mild ridicule on a word-of-mouth basis.

The Power of Thinking and of Information

The emphasis on design and creative thinking in the positive revolution means that there will be new and better approaches to problems. Here we have the power of better ideas.

Instead of the crude power of destruction there will be the unbalancing power of carefully directed effort. In the combat skill of judo the power of the opponent is not blocked but that power is used to unbalance and overcome the opponent. By well-timed rocking a heavy stone may be toppled over. The creative thinker will go on thinking until a usable solution is found.

The positive revolution puts a lot of emphasis on information and networks of information between individuals and between the circles. Information is power, just as ignorance is weakness. If you know how to do something you can do it. If you know what you are dealing with then your actions will be more appropriate.

The attitudes of the positive revolution mean that a difficult task becomes a challenge. A challenge is not a signal for despair but a signal for more information and better thinking.

We live in an information age and any group that learns to use information effectively – through better perception and thinking – is going to be in a very powerful position.

Members of the positive revolution are not crippled by old ways of thinking

The Power of Coordination and Alignment

A magnet becomes a magnet when all the little magnets within the metal come to point in the same direction (see page 6). Even if small amounts of energy are coordinated the effect may be very powerful.

If every consumer makes a particular type of consumer choice then the overall effect may be devastating. If everyone decides not to shop at a store with excessive prices then the store goes out of business. The power of consumerism and boycotts can bring about changes if used in a constructive way. Without consumers there is no selling.

In India, Gandhi used mass coordination as the main power for his movement of passive resistance.

In some cases (like a boycott) the power of coordination is used in a negative way. But that power can equally be used in a positive way. Instead of boycotting a particular store consumers can prefer to shop where they perceive good value. It is this positive use of coordination and alignment that is more in keeping with the positive revolution.

Members of the positive revolution may choose to campaign for a political candidate who has a constructive and positive attitude.

The Power of Support

In a democracy the threat of switching votes or the possibility of gaining votes strongly influences the behaviour of politicians. When the positive revolution takes hold it will no longer be enough for politicians to gain points through attack or being negative. Politicians will be expected to be constructive. There is no hurry for the positive revolution to have its own political candidates. To begin with there is more power in influencing all other candidates.

The concepts of the positive revolution allow all those people with positive and constructive attitudes to become aligned as a group. This need not be a formal alignment but candidates for political office can be looked at through the perceptions of the positive revolution and democratic choices made accordingly.

Any significant bloc of votes is very important to a political candidate so the power of this 'positive bloc' could be out of proportion to its size.

The choice of campaigning for a candidate has already been mentioned.

It is much better that members of the positive revolution do not seek political power directly as a 'yellow party' but continue to distribute their support among other parties. This is because a specific party would remove the multiplying effect of the power of support.

The positive revolution should never be permanently aligned with any one political group. Individuals may be supported according to their positive and constructive behaviour. Permanent alignment destroys the universality of the positive revolution.

Candidates for office can be asked directly whether they support the principle of the positive revolution and what they are going to do about it. A pledge of this sort can make a promise more permanent.

The Power of Spreading

The ultimate power of the positive revolution is the power of spreading.

When most people have joined the positive revolution then the positive and constructive attitudes and the creative thinking can be applied towards the improvement of society.

When most people understand and accept the five fundamental principles of the positive revolution then society will already be a better place.

So the power of spreading is the ultimate power.

The power of spreading of the positive revolution depends on many things.

There is the value of the constructive concepts and the willingness of able people to understand and to endorse these concepts.

There is the alignment of existing groups with these concepts.

There is spread through word-of-mouth and activities of the circles.

There is spread through the yellow book, the symbols, the new names and through the media.

The Power of Water

There is the power of rocks and missiles and explosives and then there is the power of water.

The power of water is slow but over time it can erode vast areas and deep canyons – a little bit at a time.

Water adapts itself to the existing terrain but still continues to exert its power. The power of water can be harnessed for constructive purposes like hydroelectric projects and canals for irrigation and rivers for navigation.

Water is needed for all living things.

The power of the positive revolution is like the power of water.

A few drops of rain over a large area eventually collects into a mighty river. Each drop makes only a small contribution.

16 SECTORS OF SOCIETY

The positive revolution is people-based. More than that, the positive revolution is based on individuals. Each individual in his or her heart and actions takes part in the positive revolution. Individuals may come together to form groups or circles in order to make their contributions even more effective.

The positive revolution is not aligned with any particular sector of society and should avoid any such specific alignment which would restrict the universality of the positive revolution.

Nevertheless the positive revolution takes place in a society in which there already exist certain defined sectors. It is therefore useful to see how the aims and methods of the positive revolution might fit the aims and methods of these other sectors.

Although the power of the positive revolution is the power of individual people, the spread of the positive revolution can be hastened or delayed by the attitudes of different sectors of society. In order to prevent misunderstanding it is necessary to make clear how the positive revolution relates to some of these sectors in society.

Any established sector of society may stand back and wait to see what happens to the positive revolution. Other reactions might include: opposing the revolution; endorsing the revolution; or ignoring the revolution.

What must be remembered is that the positive revolution is a powerful investment opportunity for society and if the opportunity is ignored it may not come round again.

The positive revolution does not seek to further the aims of any one sector of society but it furthers the aims of all those sectors that seek the improvement of society for the benefit of all the people living in that society. That is a broad objective.

The positive revolution has no enemies because it does not need enemies. The energy of the positive revolution is not obtained by defining, hating, attacking and destroying an enemy.

The following sectors will be considered:

- Older people
- Younger people
- Media
- Business
- Art
- Trade unions
- Political parties
- Other revolutionary groups

Older People

As people get older and retire they find they have more time, but suddenly their role in society collapses. Suddenly they become spectators in the game of life instead of players.

This is a pity because older people have a wisdom and experience which younger people have not yet acquired.

Older people still have a need to be involved and to feel important. The positive revolution is an ideal way for this to be achieved. As they retire from an active working life, older people can become involved in the 'contributing' life of the positive revolution.

Younger people may have the will and the energy to contribute to the positive revolution, but not the time. Older people can supply that very valuable commodity of time. To this is added wisdom and practical experience which are important for getting things done.

Older people, however, need to guard against being negative and apathetic and against the feeling that 'nothing can be done'.

Older people will benefit directly from the 'respect' aspect of the positive revolution. Older people will often benefit through being on the receiving end of the 'contribution' aspect of the positive revolution since many forms of contribution will involve helping older people. Older people have the time for self-improvement and for education. In the area of education older people are in a fine position to pass on their knowledge and in so doing to feel useful in building a better society.

The positive revolution can provide the structures in which all these things can happen – through people setting out to make it happen.

Older people also set values in society. Older people are also great communicators because they have more time to communicate.

The main point is that the positive revolution gives to older people an opportunity to contribute, usefully, to society even more actively than when they were younger.

Older people are unlikely to get involved in the bullets and bombs of traditional revolutions, but there is no aspect or activity of the positive revolution in which older people cannot get involved. This includes both active contribution and also the exercise of that vote which is every bit as powerful as the vote of a younger person.

In many countries the shift is towards an older population. So older people are going to get more political power. The positive revolution is an ideal way in which this power can be exerted in a constructive fashion.

Younger People

Young people are either bored or they are busy. They have time and energy and want to do something with them.

The easiest thing to do is to fill the time with friends, with music, with eating, with television, with social media. Time does get filled. Time does pass. Soon they have families and responsibilities and all the time and energy is taken up with surviving and earning a living.

Young people have a sense of mission and a sense of frustration. They want to do things. They want to do things to make society a better place. But there is no way of doing anything. The adults have all the levers of power. Perhaps a young person is old enough to have a vote but that cannot be used very often and is very indirect.

Young people are impatient.

It is for all these reasons that young people sometimes find an excitement and a sense of mission in traditional destructive revolutions.

Young people like to work in groups for this is a way of seeing more of your friends and making new friends.

The positive revolution is a framework for using this energy and need for mission amongst young people. With this framework young people can set up 'action groups' to design and carry out specific contributions. These become the yellow circles mentioned on page 73.

Youngsters work together in these circles to seek out areas of need and to plan and carry out their contribution. In this way youngsters get a sense of involvement, achievement and responsibility.

They find that 'doing things' can be just as much fun as sitting around filling in time.

Fashions spread extremely rapidly among young people. The wearing of yellow armbands (or wristbands) would quickly spread among young people and with it the message of the positive revolution. The category-naming language would also quickly catch on amongst them. Those values would then remain with them for life.

The framework of the positive revolution is a way youngsters can feel that they are improving society in a tangible, step-by-step way. That is important. Instead of waiting for the great revolution or drifting into apathy ('nothing can be done') young people can design and take small constructive steps that are visible.

So for young people the positive revolution is not just a mission but a form of activity and an entertainment.

Media

The media (the internet, press, radio, television) should play the leading role in the positive revolution.

There are those in the media who would like to see the media play a more serious role in society than a 'bag of sweets'. A bag of sweets is something into which you dip your hand when you want some moments of amusement. There is this trivial day-to-day role of the media to provide amusement on demand.

Then there is a bigger vision of the media as the most powerful force for change in society.

Traditionally the media has focused on controversy, fights, arguments, scandals and criticism as a way of changing society. This is because such things are naturally interesting in themselves. The result has been to accentuate the polarized nature of society and also the sense of dissatisfaction. Complaint and criticism are much easier than constructive action. It is always possible to criticize anything if you have that in mind.

But there are within the media individual editors and journalists who would like to play a more positive role in improving society.

The positive revolution provides such a framework for constructive effort.

The media could pinpoint the areas in society that need constructive contribution.

The media could highlight the activity of constructive individuals and groups and show how these people are doing things.

The media could watch and follow self-help projects.

Websites and television could run special 'yellow programs' which are designed for constructive new ideas and ways of doing things.

The media could run 'basic' education programmes including, for example, thinking skill lessons – which can easily be taught online or through television.

The media could spread directly the positive and constructive attitudes of the positive revolution.

All this is rather more important than being a 'bag of sweets'. But it is a challenge to those who work with and run the media.

The media can set values through humour, cartoons, soap operas, blogs, social media and other established mechanisms.

Business

At some point wealth has to be created before it can be distributed and enjoyed.

The constructive and positive attitudes of the positive revolution emphasize this point.

In the positive revolution, instead of demand, complaint and attack there is the concept of contribution.

There have been, and still are, greed and exploitation in business. These things can be controlled, not by an outright attack on the concept of business or on the principle of reward for organization and risk-taking, but by information, the power of united consumer action and the concept of contribution.

Business must be willing to spell out its existing contribution and its growing contribution. That is its best protection against destructive forces.

The positive revolution is interested in doing things and making things happen. The positive revolution is interested in creativity, design and effective action. All these things are the very essence of business activity itself. Business seeks to create, design, add value and be effective.

The quality circles of the positive revolution are a direct and specific way in which people can take an interest in their own jobs and seek to improve these jobs. Business should cooperate in setting up such circles and paying attention to what comes out of them.

Business needs workers. The better the quality of the workers the more effective the business may be. The emphasis in the revolution on self-improvement and on education is directly in the interests of business. The very strong emphasis on 'effectiveness' (the first fundamental principle, the 'thumb' on the hand) provides the most valuable asset which any business can ask for.

It is very much in the self-interest of business to see that its own purpose in society and the purpose of the positive revolution are parallel.

In most countries throughout the world the irresponsible and exploiting aspects of business are being curbed through information, legislation and social pressures. Business has its place in society so long as it continues to operate as a major contributor.

It is the productive values of business that are important in raising the general standard of living. Speculation and money-manipulation with the sole purpose of getting richer do not have a high value in the positive revolution. In the future the organization and thinking power that are present in business will also be needed to cope with many problems, such as pollution. Business will need to be more active and not just look after its own direct interests. Contribution needs to take over from selfishness. The more power, the more the potential for contribution.

Art

Like the media, art has a key role to play in the positive revolution. But, also like the media, it is not an easy role.

Just as the media enjoys controversy and argument so does art enjoy the extremes of human emotion. Traditionally there has been the glory of war and the sacrifices of revolution.

Because extremes of action involve extremes of emotion, war and destruction have been a natural feeding ground for art.

But there is also another side of art. This is the art of the simple, the art of ordinary people doing ordinary things, the beauty of the human spirit. This is much more difficult because it can so easily become dull. There is not the intrinsic excitement of drama and great emotions, so more is demanded of the artist. Van Gogh could paint a simple chair or some ordinary flowers as masterpieces of art. The old masters could paint family scenes or a mother with a child.

The purpose of art is to capture the spirit of a revolution, to crystallize that spirit and to carry it forward. The purpose of art is to reflect new emerging values and to define the new heroes and heroines so that people can absorb them into their perceptions.

Art should be able to do this with the positive revolution. The new idioms required give new opportunities and new challenges to artists.

Trade Unions

Historically trade unions were set up to protect the rights of the workers against the early capitalists. This function was extremely valuable because in those days (and sometimes today) the interests of the capitalist were opposite to those of the worker: for example, keep costs down and increase profits.

Today unions often have two parallel roles. One role is to continue to represent the interests of workers. The second role is to serve almost as a political party that has its own agenda for social change.

When a union presses for a wage increase several things can happen. It may be a need to catch up with wage increases in other areas. It may be a need to catch up with the cost of living. It may be a desire to have a fair share of the profits that are being made. It may be an attempt to get as high a wage as possible in the knowledge that this increase will ultimately be paid by the consumer through higher prices.

All these are legitimate ambitions. But there is a balance point at which the same pressure for higher wages is no longer in the interests of the workers. Beyond that point the business might have to raise its price so much that it becomes uncompetitive and loses market share. Beyond that point the profits become so low that further investment in the business by the owners or outside investors is not worthwhile, the infrastructure is not modernized and eventually the business closes. Beyond that point general demands for wages and the effect in higher prices can cause one type of inflation in which everyone suffers.

In the traditional antagonistic model, the union continues to press as hard as it can, management resists as hard as it can and eventually some balance point is reached.

In some unions and in some countries there has been a shift from the traditional antagonistic model to the constructive model. Both management and unions come to see that the business is there to serve four groups: investors, workers, management and consumers.

What is sometimes required is a shift, on the side of both management and unions, from the attack/defend model to constructive change.

The positive revolution provides an opportunity for unions to increase their role in representing the true interests of their members. The central concept of contribution requires workers to do a good job and management to pay workers fairly.

The creative and design aspects of the new thinking of the positive revolution provide a better means for working out new contracts and solving disputes.

The emphasis on self-improvement, education and effectiveness is directly in the interests of individual workers and also directly in the interests of the unions, because better workers mean higher productivity and a sound basis for requesting higher wages.

Quality circles are also a way of getting higher productivity which means higher wages and a more secure future in the marketplace.

In a highly competitive world in which no one owes a living to anyone else, the destructive model of union behaviour has become less relevant. There is a general move to the constructive model. But, as always, unions have to be on their guard against exploitation.

Political Parties

Every political party will claim that its ultimate purpose is the improvement of society for the benefit of the people in society. They may add that this is to be done through raising the standards of living and preserving law and order.

Where the parties would disagree is on values, policies and on bringing about this improvement, and which people are most competent to be in power.

This is an ideal picture. There are probably some politicians who want to be in power for the sake of being in power. They enjoy playing the political game for its own sake. There are some politicians who feel they have been elected solely to represent the interests of their own constituency and have no interest in the general improvement of society. There are politicians who are only interested in one specific issue, such as the environment or agriculture. There are politicians representing very deprived areas.

Nevertheless we can see if there might be agreement across all political parties on some basic assumptions:

- Can we assume that the country would work better if people were constructive rather than destructive?
- Can we assume that the country would work better if people contributed rather than complained?
- Can we assume that the country would work better if people were effective rather than ineffective?
- Can we assume that the country would work better if people were educated rather than uneducated?
- Can we assume that the country would work better if people were creative rather than critical?
- Can we assume that the country would work better if people supported the most constructive politicians?

There are special cases where we can disagree with the above assumptions. For example, if we are facing massive corruption it is better to be critical rather than creative (though we could be creative in finding ways to stop it). There are many other special cases. In general, however, any political party which did not agree with the above assumptions would have to explain why it did not agree.

A political party that believed it to be better if people were uneducated rather than educated would have to explain this belief. Perhaps it would be because people who were uneducated were easier to lead and easier to fool.

All the above assumptions also make for economic development since this depends on constructive attitudes. We can assume that all political parties would want to benefit from a baseline of growing economic development.

Since the principles of the positive revolution are so broad, so constructive and so positive it can be assumed that all political parties would want to support the positive revolution.

Where a particular political party does not want to support the positive revolution it is now legitimate to ask that party to explain why it does not want to support the attitudes of the positive revolution.

Note that the positive revolution does not arise from any particular political party, sector or group within the country. If this had been the case then a political party might have opposed it on the grounds that it was founded by an opposing party.

For all these reasons it is in the interests of all political parties to support the positive revolution.

Other Revolutionary Groups

There are other revolutionary groups that have the same overall aim of improving society for the benefit of the people in society.

Such groups may have different value systems with which to define a 'better society'.

Such groups may feel that society can only get better if certain institutions and establishments are destroyed.

Most of all, such groups will differ not in the ultimate objective but in the means of getting there.

Traditional revolutionary groups will work in the traditional dialectic way by defining the enemy. The enemy is then to be hated, attacked and destroyed. Only then can a just society be set up. The period of struggle may be long. The period of struggle may be full of hardship and suffering and bloodshed. But the end is worth it. The harder the struggle the more worthwhile the end must seem to be. The struggle becomes almost an end in itself. The struggle gives a sense of belonging, a commitment, a mission and a way of making decisions. The struggle gives a value system.

Most revolutionaries have some characteristics in common. These include vision, commitment, missions and a willingness to take action.

The two key questions are as follows:

1. Do traditional revolutionaries enjoy hate, attack and destruction for their own sake or only as a means to the desired end?
2. Do traditional revolutionaries choose the method of hate, attack and destruction because it has been the only model of revolution that is available?

If the choice of the traditional method of revolution is because this was the only choice available for those who wanted to change society, then the positive revolution can provide a new choice.

A true revolutionary might find this new choice attractive in its advantages and practicality. Such a revolutionary might switch his or her own talents and commitment to the new style of revolution.

17 PROBLEMS

There are problems of poverty. There are problems of ill health. There are problems of inner-city decay. There are problems of crime, violence, law and order. There are problems of environmental pollution. There are problems of industrial competition.

There are any number of problems and it is possible to address each problem and to find solutions. This is being done and sometimes solutions are indeed found. But there are many who feel that these piecemeal solutions take too long to find and are inadequate.

In the end the fundamental culture and attitude of a society are as important as quick-fix problem-solving. If the attitude is right and the constructive habits are in place, then problem-solving is much easier. The negative attitude is useful for pointing out the problems but much less useful for solving them. A few problems can be solved by simple removal of something that is causing distress. If you are sitting on a pin you remove the pin and all is well. Most problems are much more complex and it is not a matter of removing an annoyance. Most problems require a constructive, creative and design approach. It is not a matter of pretending to have the right answer while your political opponent has the wrong answer. Very often there is no right answer and both parties need to work together to find answers. The to and fro of traditional politics is sometimes seen to be a sort of pantomime which follows the rituals laid down for it.

So there is a yearning for more positive and more constructive thinking. That is what the positive revolution is about. The positive revolution will not instantly solve all problems but it will provide a better basis for the solution of problems and also the design for a better future. The positive revolution will also involve people in working towards this better future – instead of believing that complaint is a sufficient contribution.

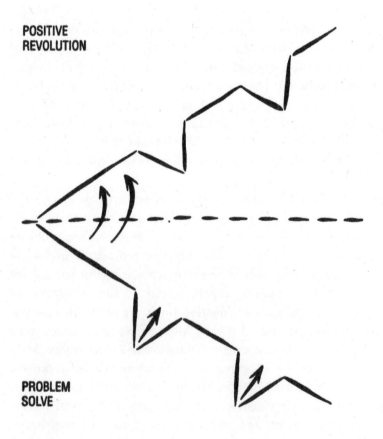

POSITIVE
REVOLUTION

PROBLEM
SOLVE

SUMMARY

This is a personal handbook for a positive revolution. The book is short because it is intended to be practical. The book puts forward the principles and the methods of the positive revolution.

Traditional revolutions are negative and seek to improve society through the definition of enemies who can then be hated, attacked and overthrown.

The positive revolution has no enemies. The positive revolution has no central organization and no dogma. The positive revolution is based on individual people, their attitudes and their perceptions.

Everyone can become a member of the positive revolution. Individuals can work on their own or come together as groups to use the power of organization to make their contributions more effective.

As in rainfall, tiny contributions come together to give a powerful river that in time sculpts the landscape.

The positive revolution is to be enjoyed as it is happening. It is not a sacrifice for some ultimate goal but positive and constructive steps forward, one after the other. Each point reached is a goal that sets a new goal.

The symbols of the revolution are the colour yellow and the outline of the hand with spread fingers. The five basic principles of the positive revolution are represented by the fingers:

THUMB: represents 'effectiveness'. Without the thumb the hand does not work. Without effectiveness there is no revolution.

INDEX FINGER: represents 'constructive'. The index finger points the way forward, the direction to follow. This direction is constructive and positive.

SECOND FINGER: represents 'respect' and human values. This is the longest finger since respect and human values are more important than anything else.

THIRD FINGER: represents 'self-improvement'. This is the individual working on himself or herself to become a little bit better each day. Better people make better revolutions.

LITTLE FINGER: represents 'contribution'. The little finger is small but it symbolizes that a contribution is valuable no matter how small it may be. Small contributions add up to great effects.

The hand is always with you to remind you of the principles of the positive revolution.

The positive revolution uses perception rather than bullets and bombs. Perception changes values and changes the way we see people. To help perception a framework of classification is provided. We can then see people through that framework. There are four positive categories and four negative categories with a neutral category in the middle:

CATEGORY ONE: Leader and organizer. Not only contributes but makes it possible for others to contribute in a constructive and effective way.

CATEGORY TWO: A major individual contributor but without the multiplying effect of category one.

CATEGORY THREE: Hard-working, cooperative and helpful. Motivated and tries hard even though eventual contribution may not be major.

CATEGORY FOUR: Positive, agreeable, pleasant and cheer-ful. Does a job well enough and is nice to have around. Not very effective or even motivated to be effective.

CATEGORY FIVE: Neutral and passive. Content to drift from moment to moment. Fills in the time with pleasures and distractions.

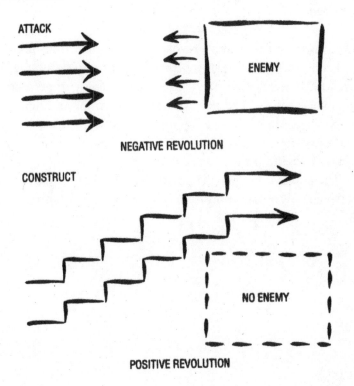

CATEGORY SIX: Critical, negative and destructive. Such a person uses his or her intelligence to attack rather than to build. May mean well.

CATEGORY SEVEN: Behaviour that is totally selfish. Such a person is not seeking to hurt others but is concerned solely with his or her own interests.

CATEGORY EIGHT: The bully who uses his or her own power to get what is wanted from others. The deliberate exploitation of other people.

CATEGORY NINE: The psychopath who has no respect whatever for the rights or existence of others. No morals and no conscience.

The power of the positive revolution will come from positive and constructive attitudes together with an emphasis on effectiveness. Power will also come from the exercise of perception to change values. The final power comes from an alignment of all these things in a growing number of people who feel that passivity and negativity are not the best ways of moving towards a better future.

The power is not just the power of a group of people but the personal power that arises from being positive and constructive.

APPENDIX:
HOW TO RUN AN E-CLUB

An E-Club is an effectiveness club. What is effectiveness? Effectiveness is setting out to do something and then doing it. What is the purpose of an E-Club?

- Some highly intelligent people are not very effective. Perhaps their intelligence gives them doubts, fears and anxieties. Perhaps there is the paralysis of analysis. Yet without effectiveness that intelligence is somewhat wasted. Intelligence may be something with which you were born. But effectiveness is a skill you can develop. The E-Club is a way of developing the skill of effectiveness.

- There are people who really enjoy being effective. They like to achieve things. They want to set out to do things and then to do them. For some people effectiveness is almost a hobby. The E-Club is a place where that effectiveness can be enjoyed and also demonstrated to others.

- Many people find that the ordinary work they are doing does not provide much scope for achievement. The E-Club can afford an opportunity for achievement in an area you choose.

- Some people lead very passive lives: surfing the internet, watching television, listening to music, talking to other people, reading magazines and newspapers, looking at social media. There is very little 'doing' other than the daily chores of living. The E-Club offers a place for doing and for enjoying doing. This is particularly important for younger people and for older ones. Younger people have energy they need to use and skills they need to exercise. Older people need something to engage their intelligence and talents.
- As with any other club, the E-Club has a social aspect. Meeting people and doing things with other people is an end in itself. The E-Clubs have an active purpose instead of just meeting and talking.
- The positive revolution requires those taking part to be constructive. It is possible just to be constructive in attitude. It is even better to be constructive in action as well. The E-Club provides just such a framework for constructive action.

General Overview

An E-Club is made up of a group of people who meet periodically to set themselves action tasks and then to report on the progress of those tasks. Since effectiveness is a combination of thinking and doing, an E-Club involves thinking that designs and sets the task; thinking that plans the execution of the task; and then the doing what's necessary to carry through the task. Difficulties, problems and achievements are reported back and shared with other members of the E-Club.

An E-Club may be involved in several tasks at once. There may also be separate task forces to carry out different tasks.

The Tasks

Every E-Club compiles its own catalogue of tasks. In time the catalogues from different E-Clubs may be combined to give a major catalogue of possible tasks. Members of the E-Club conceive and design tasks. This in itself is part of effectiveness. The tasks should provide value. This value should not be at the expense of other people or of damage to the environment.

We too often assume that work is obvious and that someone can be employed to do it. But the design of work is an art in itself. What can be done that will provide value? In time there will even be a profession of 'work-packagers'. In some ways this is what an entrepreneur does. E-Clubs should not just carry out obvious tasks but should put effort into designing new ones. Some of the tasks should be easy and achievable. There is not much point in setting only impossible tasks. Skill and confidence are not built up that way.

One task that is always part of the E-Club routine is the monthly party. This task is given each month to two members of the club. These parties are not just for members of the E-Club but for outsiders, friends and potential members of the club. The parties provide a specific task that can be planned and achieved.

Report Back

At each E-Club meeting a report is made on the tasks and projects in progress. This is a key part of the progress. This report provides a sense of achievement in what has been done. The report also provides a sort of deadline for achieving something. The report may contain the following types of comment on any task:

- Void, blank, no action, nothing has been done because there has been no idea of what to do or how to start.
- Inertia, laziness and inaction, not because of difficulty in knowing what to do but because of lack of will or energy.
- Friction, resistance, difficulties. No major obstacle, but a bit like dancing in treacle.
- Report on the small steps that have been achieved, even if these are much smaller than the intended steps.
- Full achievement of the targets set.

During the feedback the other members of the club can ask questions – not in a critical manner but to explore what went wrong or how success was achieved.

People

E-Club membership can be as small as two people or as large as eight. A growing club may consist of more than eight people, but should then split into further clubs. Each member of an E-Club should seek to be a member of two clubs. First there is the E-Club of which that person is a member. Then there is the E-Club which that person sets up directly – acting as organizer. So each member is both a follower and a leader.

Time

E-Club meetings should be held once a month. The history of many organizations suggests that a definite date should be set, for example the first Monday in the month. It is better to have a set date and then to adjust this occasionally than to try each time to find a date that suits everybody.

The formal part of an E-Club meeting should take exactly two hours. During that time a member may request extra time, for instance to report back on a lengthy project or to seek thinking help on a project. This extra time takes place after the formal meeting, as a sort of appendix. The amount of time requested should be indicated. Some members of the club may be unable to be present for this extra time.

Ritual

There is a natural feeling against artificiality and formality. Yet experience has shown that organizations, and even religions, with a strong sense of ritual tend to be more successful and to last longer. This is because the ritual, meaningless as it may seem at the time, provides the momentum to keep going even when enthusiasm is temporarily absent. Ritual also enhances the sense of belonging.

Punctuality is a sort of ritual. Punctuality is also part of effectiveness. Punctuality is the simplest expression of the discipline that is necessary in thinking and action in order to focus upon what is being done. So E-Club meetings should start and end precisely at the set time.

Yellow is the colour of the positive revolution and is also the colour of the E-Clubs. Each club may choose a yellow item to have present at meetings as a token, symbol or mascot.

Statement

At the beginning of every meeting the organizer reads out the purpose of the E-Clubs. This is as follows:

'To provide a setting for the development, exercise and enjoyment of effectiveness through the designing and setting of tasks and projects and the carrying through of these tasks and projects. An E-Club may not carry out any action which is illegal or immoral or harmful to any living creature or the environment. The value of the tasks and projects must be clearly defined in advance. E-Clubs should not be used for political purposes.'

Format and Agenda

An E-Club meeting should follow the following format:

1. Opening of meeting, reading of E-Club purpose statement, apologies and explanation of absence of members. (5 minutes)
2. Direct practice of thinking skills. (20 minutes)
3. Suggestions and designs for new projects which can be added to the project catalogue. Also discussion of new projects that are to be undertaken by E-Club members. (15 minutes)
4. Reporting back of progress on existing projects. If further time is required, this is requested as a specific extension after the formal meeting has ended. (35 minutes)
5. Thinking applied to existing projects or to planning new projects. Consideration of alternatives and ways of overcoming problems. (30 minutes)
6. Formal setting of next-stage targets in existing projects and also new tasks or projects. (10 minutes)
7. Administrative details and choice of organizers for the next party. The date of the monthly party may or may not be the same as the E-Club meeting. (5 minutes)

Thinking Skills

Effectiveness is not simply a matter of energy and action. Thinking is also required. This is not just argument or analysis but the thinking for action that I once called 'operacy'. There can be practice in the use of the 'six hats' method (see page 88 and my book *Six Thinking Hats* (Penguin Life, 2016)); use of the CoRT thinking program (www.cortthinking.com); use of lateral thinking techniques *(Lateral Thinking* (Penguin Life, 2016)) or *How to Have Creative Ideas* (Vermilion, 2007).

The Organizer

There is only one formal official in an E-Club. This is the organizer. This is often the person who set up the E-Club in the first place, but the role may pass to another if the initiator is not effective enough as organizer. The organizer arranges the meeting and ensures that the timetable is adhered to. The organizer may delegate functions to other members of the club. The organizer role is a permanent one, but the organizer can be changed at any time if two-thirds of the members of the club wish to make such a change.

Log Book

A formal log book or minutes of the meeting should be kept. These need not go into great detail. Those involved in a project or task can supply a more detailed report which is then made part of the log book. The log book should record the date of the meeting, the people present and the headings of the subjects treated at the meeting.

Achievement Score

An achievement score for projects is not necessary, but for those who want to use one, here is a suggestion:

Points out of a maximum of 20 are awarded for the following:

- Importance of the task or project (includes value).
- Degree of completion.
- Completion on schedule.
- Difficulty of the task or project.
- Enjoyment of carrying through the task or project.

Laziness

The purpose of E-Clubs is to provide a forum for people to be effective. If members are ineffective through laziness or inertia there is no point in having them in the club. So any member who misses two consecutive meetings is automatically dropped from membership of the club unless there is good reason for this absence, such as illness or travel.

Register

I shall be setting up a register of active E-Clubs. No E-Club can apply for entry to this register until it has already held six successful meetings. The logs of these meetings may be requested. After six successful meetings an E-Club may apply for entry to the register.

Competition and Communication

When there are sufficient E-Clubs on the register, then it will be possible to organize meetings and competitions for those who want to be involved in such activities.

Further Information

Some people may feel that the information given here is inadequate. Experience has taught me that some people want more and more information and still do not do anything. The E-Clubs are for people who want to be effective. The first step in that effectiveness is to get going. Make that the first step towards being effective. I believe there is enough information to get going and to enjoy being effective.

INDEX

Page references in *italics* indicate images.

Also by Edward de Bono

Parallel Thinking

Western thinking is failing because it was not designed to deal with change

In this provocative masterpiece of creative thinking, Edward de Bono argues for a game-changing new way to think. For thousands of years we have followed the thinking system designed by the Greek philosophers Socrates, Plato and Aristotle, based on analysis and argument. But if we are to flourish in today's rapidly changing world we need to free our minds of these 'boxes' and embrace a more flexible and nimble model.

Parallel Thinking is an invaluable insight into the word of creativity; de Bono unveils unique methods of brainstorming and explains preconceived ideas of what creativity involves and is. This book is not about philosophy; it is about the practical (and parallel) thinking required to get things done in an ever-changing world.

In this extraordinarily prescient book Edward de Bono sets out his method for achieving the ultimate 21st century goal: work-life balance.

Defined in terms of life-space and self-space, de Bono invites the reader to look at their life and measure the gap between these spaces – the smaller the gap, the greater our chances at happiness; but if the life-space is vastly bigger than the self-space, our coping ability is compromised and anxiety is likely.

For anyone concerned with happiness and life-fulfilment this book is essential reading, and is perhaps more resonant with readers now than ever before.

Five-Day Course in Thinking

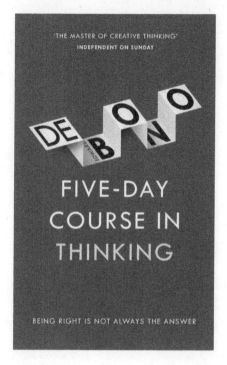

First published in 1967, this remarkable title from one of history's greatest minds remains a must-read in the world of creative thinking.

Based on the belief that an error can lead to the right decision, de Bono guides the reader through a series of problems and puzzles, all designed to help us analyse our personal style of thinking and to consider the potential methods that we never use.

There are three courses, each five days long and each created to focus on a different style of thinking. A true life-changer, this book will have you thinking in way that you never thought were possible.

Why are we more prone to be negative? And how can we become more positive, both as individuals and as a society? We need to develop new concepts: some brand new and some slightly different. We have to make a deliberate and positive effort to secure a positive future; we must harness the focused power of human thinking unleashed from its pettiness.

Since Future Positive was first published in 1979, our belief in the power of positive thinking has only deepened.

De Bono was on to something in 1979: the future is positive – if we want it to be.